CAKES & CAKE ICING

Edited by
Jo Barker

OCTOPUS

CONTENTS

This edition first published 1978 by
Octopus Books Limited
59 Grosvenor Street, London W.1.

© 1978 Octopus Books Limited

ISBN 0 7064 0698 2

Produced and printed in Hong Kong by
Mandarin Publishers Limited
22a Westlands Road, Quarry Bay

Frontispiece: FROSTED CAKE *(page 34) (Photograph: Tate and Lyle)*

Weights and Measures

All measurements in this book are based on Imperial weights and measures, with American equivalents given in parenthesis.

Measurements in *weight* in the Imperial and American system are the same. Measurements in *volume* are different, and the following table shows the equivalents:

Spoon measurements

Imperial	U.S.
1 tablespoon	1 tablespoon
1½ tablespoons	2 tablespoons
2 tablespoons	3 tablespoons
	(abbrev: T)

Level spoon measurements are used in all the recipes.

Liquid measurements

1 Imperial pint	20 fluid ounces
1 American pint	16 fluid ounces
1 American cup	8 fluid ounces

American Ingredients

Where a recipe states 'self-raising' flour American readers should use 'self-rising' flour. If this is not available, substitute all-purpose flour and add 1 teaspoon baking powder to every 1 cup of flour.

Commercially prepared 'mixed spice' is included in several recipes. If unobtainable blend together a selection of ground spices, such as nutmeg, cinnamon, mace and ginger and use instead.

INTRODUCTION

Baking cakes is one of the most fundamental yet most exciting cooking skills. It is not difficult to acquire the art of successful cake-making, providing a few simple rules are followed. One needs to understand how different ingredients combine and to appreciate the importance of such factors as oven temperatures, preparing tins and testing cakes.

Cakes are basically made from four main ingredients: fat, flour, eggs and sugar, with the exception of some whisked sponges which contain no fat. Of course numerous flavourings and additional ingredients, such as fruit, peel, nuts, chocolate and spices can be incorporated into the basic mixture to give endless variations.

Within the four basic cake ingredients there is a wide range to choose from, giving variety in flavour and texture. Butter, margarine and oil are all used in cake-making, the choice of fat depending partly on the method of preparation. Rubbed-in mixtures require hard margarine or chilled butter. Soft table margarine blends easily with other ingredients — an advantage for all-in-one cakes. However, the volume of these cakes is not as good as that obtained with softened block margarine or butter.

Softer flours are ideal for cake-making because they yield a fine, soft texture. Most cakes require a raising agent and it is essential that the correct quantity is added. Self-raising (self-rising) flour is useful because it contains a standard amount of raising agent which is evenly blended with the flour and guarantees a good result. Plain (all-purpose) flour is equally suitable for cake-making providing the correct quantity of baking powder is added. There is always the temptation to add more than the recipe states with the hope of baking a larger cake, but too much raising agent can produce disastrous results. If you only have plain (all-purpose) flour in the kitchen and a recipe suggests self-raising flour, substitute plain (all-purpose) flour and add 1 teaspoon baking powder to every 4 oz. (1 cup) flour.

There are also several types of sugar available. Castor (superfine) sugar should always be used for whisked sponges because it yields a fine, soft texture. Darker sugars have more flavour and are ideal for rich fruit cakes. The size of eggs will make a difference to the volume of a baked cake, especially to whisked or creamed mixtures.

Preparing cake tins: Cakes should be baked in tins which have been lined or greased. For lining, use greased greaseproof paper or non-stick parchment, which does not need greasing and can be re-used.

Line the sides and base of deep cake tins. For sandwich tins (cake layer pans) it is usually sufficient just to grease the tin but for extra precaution against sticking, place a round of lining paper on the base. For fatless sponges and Genoese sponges sprinkle the greased tin with flour to give the sponge a crisp outer edge.

Testing whether a cake is cooked: Cakes should be well-risen, golden brown and slightly shrunk from the sides of the tin. To test a sponge or creamed cake, press the top lightly with the fingertips. The cake should spring back, leaving no impression, if it is cooked. For a large deep cake, such as a rich fruit cake, insert a warm skewer into the centre. If the cake is cooked, the skewer should come out quite clean.

Decorating cakes: Most home-baked cakes are delicious eaten plain but iced and tastefully decorated they look more attractive and taste even better. Decorations need not be elaborate — often the simple designs are most effective. In this book you will find recipes for a variety of fillings, icings and toppings. Ideas range from buttercreams and fudge frostings to feather icing, flavoured glacé icings and royal icing. There is unlimited scope for trying out fillings and toppings on different cakes and experimenting with flavours and colourings.

Storage: Cakes should be kept in air-tight tins or similar containers until required. Storage times depend on the type of cake. Fatless sponges should be eaten on the day they are prepared. Creamed cakes will usually keep for up to 1 week. Fruit cakes will keep for several months but should be wrapped in foil before storing in a tightly sealed polythene bag or airtight tin.

CHRISTMAS CAKE *(page 42)*

UNBAKED CAKES

Unbaked cakes should be made the day before required and chilled. They are best served straight from the refrigerator.

Chestnut Cake

15½ oz. can unsweetened
  chestnut purée or 1½ lb.
  (4½ cups) chestnuts
8 oz. (8 squares) plain
  (semi-sweet) chocolate
4 oz. (½ cup) butter, softened

4 oz. (½ cup) castor (superfine)
  sugar
few drops of vanilla essence
  (extract)
¼ pint (⅔ cup) double (heavy)
  cream, whipped

If using fresh chestnuts, blanch in boiling water, cool slightly then peel away the skins. Place the chestnuts in a saucepan and add ½ pint (1¼ cups) water. Bring to the boil then simmer until tender. Drain then sieve or reduce to a purée in an electric blender.

Line a 1 lb. loaf tin with greased greaseproof paper or non-stick parchment. Melt the chocolate in a bowl over hot water. Cool slightly. Cream the butter with the sugar until pale and fluffy. Beat in the chestnut purée, vanilla essence and cooled melted chocolate.

Turn into prepared tin. Refrigerate overnight. Decorate with whipped cream and leave in the refrigerator until required. Slice before serving.
Makes 8-10 slices

Belgian Fudge Cake

4 oz. (½ cup) butter
2 tablespoons (3T) golden
 (maple) syrup
8 oz. (2 cups) biscuits, crushed
1 oz. (2T) seedless raisins
2 oz. (¼ cup) glacé (candied)
 cherries, quartered
5 oz. (5 squares) plain
 (semi-sweet) chocolate, chopped
Fudge icing:
2 oz. (2 squares) plain
 (semi-sweet) chocolate

1 oz. (2T) butter
2 tablespoons (3T) water
6 oz. (1⅓ cups) icing
 (confectioners') sugar, sifted
Decoration:
1 oz. (¼ cup) blanched almonds,
 chopped
glacé (candied) cherries, halved
angelica diamonds

Line a 1 lb. loaf tin with greased greaseproof paper or non-stick parchment. Gently melt the butter and syrup in a saucepan over low heat. Remove from the heat and stir in the crushed biscuits, raisins, cherries and chocolate. Press firmly into the prepared tin and leave in the refrigerator to set.

To make the icing, melt the chocolate and butter with the water in a saucepan over a very low heat. Remove from the heat and stir in the icing sugar. Beat until cool and thick.

When the cake has set, cut into 3 layers. Sandwich these layers together with the icing and spread a layer of icing over the top of the cake. Decorate with chopped nuts, cherries and angelica diamonds. Serve chilled.
Serves 6-8

Refrigerated Coffee Cake

4 oz. (½ cup) butter
6 oz. (1⅓ cups) icing
 (confectioners') sugar, sifted
1 egg, separated
½ teaspoon coffee essence (strong
 black coffee)

1 tablespoon cocoa powder, sifted
6 tablespoons (½ cup) strong
 black coffee
40 petit beurre or other oblong
 biscuits
6 blanched almonds, split

Cream the butter until soft and gradually work in the icing sugar and egg yolk. Blend in the coffee essence and the cocoa. Beat the egg white until stiff and fold into the mixture.

Dip 10 biscuits in the coffee and arrange close together in two rows on an oblong plate. Spread with a layer of icing. Continue these layers. Spread icing over top and sides of the cake. Pipe rosettes of icing on top of the cake and decorate with split blanched almonds. Refrigerate before cutting.
Makes 10-12 slices

11

Chocolate Crunch

2 oz. (3T) golden (maple) syrup
3 oz. (⅓ cup) margarine
1 oz. (2T) castor (superfine) sugar
2 tablespoons (3T) cocoa powder
8 oz. (2 cups) digestive biscuits
  (graham crackers), crushed

1 tablespoon brandy or rum
Icing:
2 oz. (2 squares) plain
  (semi-sweet) chocolate

Thoroughly grease a 6 or 7 inch round loose-bottomed cake tin. Melt the syrup, margarine and sugar in a saucepan over low heat. Add the cocoa and mix well. Remove from heat and stir in the crushed biscuit and brandy or rum. Press into the prepared tin. Chill.

Melt the chocolate in a bowl over a pan of hot water and spread over the cake. Smooth the surface or mark a pattern with a fork. Leave for at least 4 hours in a refrigerator to set. Cut into slices before serving.

Makes one 6 or 7 inch round cake

Sky Rockets

2½ oz. (⅓ cup) digestive biscuits
  (graham crackers), crushed
3 oz. (½ cup) dates, stoned
  (pitted) and chopped
2 oz. (⅓ cup) currants
1½ oz. (3T) glacé (candied)
  cherries, chopped

3 tablespoons (¼ cup) apricot jam
8 oz. packet marzipan
orange and green food colouring
8 lollipop or similar sticks
few silver and gold balls
few small sweets

Mix together the biscuit crumbs, dates, currants and cherries. Bind together with jam. Divide into 8 pieces and shape each into a barrel with one pointed end.

Colour three-quarters of the marzipan orange and the remaining quarter green. Roll the orange marzipan out on a sugared board. Divide into 8 pieces and wrap around each barrel. Roll out the green marzipan and use to make the pointed end of the rocket. Impale each rocket on a stick and decorate with silver and gold balls and small sweets.

Makes 8

These novelty cakes are ideal for a children's party. Vary the colourings, as liked.

CHOCOLATE CRUNCH *(Photograph: Tate and Lyle)*

Cream Treat

2 oz. (¼ cup) margarine
3 tablespoons (¼ cup) golden
  (maple) syrup
6 digestive biscuits (graham
  crackers)
2 tablespoons (3T) cocoa powder
2 large eggs, beaten

few drops of vanilla essence
  (extract)
2 oz. (⅓ cup) seedless raisins
¼ pint (⅔ cup) double (heavy)
  cream, whipped
grated chocolate to decorate

Line a 6 inch sandwich tin (cake layer pan) with greased greaseproof paper
or non-stick parchment. Melt the margarine and syrup in a saucepan.
Cool. Crush the biscuits and mix with the cocoa. Beat the eggs and vanilla
essence into the melted mixture. Stir in the biscuits, cocoa and raisins.

Spread into the prepared tin but do not press down too firmly. Leave in
the refrigerator for about 2 hours to set.

Turn the cake out onto a serving plate. Decorate with whipped cream
and sprinkle with grated chocolate. Keep in the refrigerator until required.
Makes one 6 inch round cake

Chocolate Log

4 oz. (½ cup) mixed glacé
  (candied) fruit (cherries, angelica
  and pineapple)
1 tablespoon brandy
2 oz. (2 squares) plain
  (semi-sweet) chocolate, grated
8 oz. (2 cups) cake crumbs
8 oz. (1 cup) cottage cheese,
  sieved
4 oz. (½ cup) cream cheese
1 oz. (2T) castor (superfine) sugar

Icing and decoration:
2 oz. (2 squares) plain
  (semi-sweet) chocolate
¼ pint (⅔ cup) double (heavy)
  cream
christmas cake decorations (holly,
  robins, snowmen etc.)
icing (confectioners') sugar for
  dusting

Marinate the fruit in brandy for at least 30 minutes then chop. Line an
11 × 7 inch Swiss (jelly) roll tin with greased greaseproof paper or
non-stick parchment. Combine the grated chocolate, cake crumbs,
cheeses, sugar and chopped fruit, and mix thoroughly.

Spread the mixture onto the lining paper and roll up like a Swiss (jelly)
roll, using the paper as a guide but do not roll it inside the mixture. Leave in
a refrigerator to set; about 3-4 hours.

To make the icing, melt the chocolate in a bowl over hot water. Cool.
Whisk cream until just thick and fold in the cooled, melted chocolate.

Place the cake on a serving dish and spread with the chocolate cream.
Mark with a fork to give a log effect. Decorate and dust with sifted icing
sugar. Chill before serving.
Makes one log

Mocha Brandy Slice

4 oz. (4 squares) plain
  (semi-sweet) chocolate
4 oz. (½ cup) margarine
4 oz. (½ cup) castor (superfine)
  sugar
1 tablespoon instant coffee
  powder

6 tablespoons (½ cup) boiling water
1 tablespoon brandy
36 petit beurre or other oblong
  biscuits
2 oz. (½ cup) slivered almonds
4 glacé (candied) cherries, halved
16 angelica leaves

Melt the chocolate in a bowl over a saucepan of hot water. Cool slightly. Cream the margarine and sugar together until pale and fluffy. Beat in the melted chocolate.

Dissolve the coffee powder in the boiling water in a shallow dish and add the brandy. Dip 6 biscuits in the liquid then arrange on an oblong serving dish to form a rectangular base. Spread with a thin layer of chocolate cream. Continue with these layers until all the biscuits have been used.

Spread top and sides with the remaining chocolate cream. Press slivered almonds to the sides. Decorate the top with cherries and angelica. Keep refrigerated until required.

Makes 10-12 slices

Hazelnut Wafer Cake

3 oz. (⅓ cup) sugar
4 tablespoons (⅓ cup) water
3 egg yolks, beaten
8 oz. (1 cup) unsalted (sweet)
  butter
2 oz. (⅓ cup) hazelnuts (filberts),
  browned and finely grated
8-10 continental fan wafers
6 tablespoons (½ cup) raspberry
  jam (approximately)

Icing:
3 oz. (½ cup) plain (semi-sweet)
  chocolate pieces
4 tablespoons (⅓ cup) water
8 oz. (1¾ cups) icing
  (confectioners') sugar, sifted
½ teaspoon salad oil
2-3 drops vanilla essence (extract)

Dissolve the sugar in the water over moderate heat. Bring to the boil and boil the syrup until a sugar thermometer registers 230°F or until a little of the cooled syrup will form a thread when drawn between the thumb and forefinger. Pour onto the egg yolks and whisk until thick. Cream the butter and gradually beat in the syrup and egg mixture to give a smooth filling, then stir in the nuts.

Sandwich the wafers together with layers of jam and filling to form a wafer cake. Stand the cake on a wire rack with a plate underneath. To make the icing, place the chocolate and water in a bowl over hot water. Stir until the chocolate has melted. Beat in the icing sugar, oil and vanilla essence. Pour over the cake and leave to set.

Makes one wafer cake

ONE-STAGE CAKES

Cakes made by the all-in-one method require softened margarine or butter and slightly more raising agent than those prepared by the conventional method. The mixture can be made and stored in the refrigerator overnight before baking, if necessary.

Catherine Wheel

8 oz. (1 cup) margarine, softened
8 oz. (1 cup) castor (superfine) sugar
4 large eggs
7 oz. (1¾ cups) self-raising flour
1 teaspoon baking powder
1½ oz. (⅓ cup) cocoa powder
Icing and decoration:
4 oz. (½ cup) soft margarine
few drops of vanilla essence (extract)

12 oz. (2⅔ cups) icing (confectioners') sugar (approximately), sifted
2 tablespoons (3T) evaporated milk
4 oz. (⅔ cup) mixed dried fruit (sultanas, dates, apricots, raisins and currants)
pink and green food colouring
candles and candle holders
silver and gold balls
few small sweets

Line a 10 inch round cake tin with greased greaseproof paper or non-stick parchment. Combine the cake ingredients together in a mixing bowl. Beat thoroughly with a wooden spoon for 1-2 minutes until mixture is smooth. Turn into prepared tin and smooth the top.

Bake just above the centre of a moderate oven, 350°F, Gas Mark 4 for 40-50 minutes or until the cake is springy to the touch and has shrunk slightly from the edge of the tin. Turn out onto a wire rack to cool. Cut the cake into 2 layers.

Cream together the margarine and vanilla essence for the icing. Beat in half the icing sugar and the evaporated milk. Add the remaining icing sugar gradually, beating to give a smooth, coating consistency.

Add half the mixed fruit to one third of the icing and use to sandwich the cake layers together. Spread icing over the top of the cake. Divide the remainder of the icing in half and colour one part pink and the other green, adding more icing sugar, if necessary, to give a piping consistency.

Decorate the top of the cake with a piped star pattern, as illustrated. Complete the decoration with mixed fruit, candles, silver and gold balls and small sweets. This cake is ideal for a children's party.
Makes one 10 inch round cake

Coffee and Sultana Novelty Ring

4 oz. (½ cup) margarine, softened
4 oz. (½ cup) castor (superfine)
  sugar
2 large eggs, beaten
6 oz. (1½ cups) self-raising flour,
  sifted
1 tablespoon coffee essence
  (strong black coffee)
1 tablespoon water (approximately)
3 oz. (½ cup) sultanas (seedless
  white raisins), chopped
1 teaspoon baking powder, sifted

Icing and decoration:
3 oz. (⅓ cup) soft margarine
8 oz. (1¾ cups) icing
  (confectioners') sugar, sifted
1 tablespoon coffee essence
  (strong black coffee)
1 tablespoon milk (approximately)
2 tablespoons (3T) sultanas
4 glacé (candied) cherries,
  quartered
surprise parcels for guests
coloured streamers

Grease an 8 inch ring mould. Mix all cake ingredients together and beat with a wooden spoon for 1-2 minutes until the mixture is light in colour. Add more water, if necessary, to give a smooth dropping consistency. Spoon into prepared tin and level the top.

Bake just above the centre of a moderate oven, 350°F, Gas Mark 4 for 35-40 minutes or until shrunk slightly from the edges of the tin and springy to the touch. Turn out and cool on a wire rack.

To make the icing, combine the margarine, icing sugar, coffee essence and milk. Beat well, adding more milk if necessary, to give a smooth icing. Place the cake on a serving plate and coat with icing. Pipe stars around the base of the cake and decorate with sultanas. Decorate top of cake with cherries. Attach streamers to parcels and pile in the centre of the cake.
Makes one 8 inch ring cake

All-in-one Fruit Cake

12 oz. (3 cups) self-raising flour
1 teaspoon mixed spice
6 oz. (¾ cup) margarine, softened
6 oz. (¾ cup) castor (superfine)
  sugar
3 eggs

3 oz. (½ cup) sultanas (seedless
  white raisins)
3 oz. (½ cup) seedless raisins
3 oz. (⅓ cup) glacé (candied)
  cherries, chopped

Line an 8 inch round cake tin with greased greaseproof paper or non-stick parchment. Sift the flour and spice into a bowl. Add the rest of the ingredients. Beat thoroughly with a wooden spoon for 1-2 minutes until the mixture is pale and smooth.

Turn into the prepared tin and bake in the centre of a moderate oven, 325°F, Gas Mark 3 for 1½-2 hours or until a skewer inserted into the centre of the cake comes out clean. If the top of the cake seems to be browning too quickly during cooking, cover with foil.

Leave the cake in the tin for 15 minutes before turning out onto a wire rack to cool.

Makes one 8 inch round cake

All-in-one Sandwich Layer Cake

4 oz. (1 cup) self-raising flour
1 teaspoon baking powder
4 oz. (½ cup) margarine, softened
4 oz. (½ cup) castor (superfine)
  sugar
2 large eggs

Filling:
2 oz. (¼ cup) margarine, softened
3 oz. (¾ cup) icing (confectioners')
  sugar, sifted
2 tablespoons (3T) lemon curd
Decoration:
1 oz. (¼ cup) icing (confectioners')
  sugar, sifted

Thoroughly grease and flour two 7 inch sandwich tins (cake layer pans). Sift the flour and baking powder into a bowl. Add the remaining cake ingredients. Beat thoroughly with a wooden spoon for 1-2 minutes or until pale and fluffy.

Divide the mixture evenly between the prepared tins and smooth the tops. Bake above the centre of a moderate oven, 350°F, Gas Mark 4 for 25-35 minutes or until slightly shrunk from the edge of the tins and springy to the touch. Turn out and cool on a wire rack.

Beat all filling ingredients together until the mixture is light and fluffy. Sandwich the cake layers together with filling. Dust the top of the cake with sifted icing sugar. Using the back of a knife blade, mark a lattice pattern across the sugar.

Makes one 7 inch round cake

Simple Celebration Cake

Sandwich Layer Cake Mixture:
8 oz. (2 cups) self-raising flour
2 teaspoons baking powder
8 oz. (1 cup) butter, softened
8 oz. (1 cup) castor (superfine)
  sugar
4 eggs
Icing:
12 oz. (1½ cups) butter, softened
1½ lb. (5¼ cups) icing
  (confectioners') sugar
finely grated rind of 1 orange
3 tablespoons (¼ cup) orange
  juice (approximately)
few drops of yellow food colouring
Decoration:
yellow roses or candles
ribbon

Prepare the mixture according to the basic recipe (see page 19). Divide the mixture between two greased and floured 8 or 9 inch sandwich tins (cake layer pans) and level the tops.

Bake above the centre of a moderate oven, 350°F, Gas Mark 4 for 30-40 minutes or until well risen and springy to the touch. Turn out carefully and cool on a wire rack.

Prepare the icing by creaming together the butter, icing sugar, orange rind and juice and the colouring.

Sandwich the cake layers together with about one quarter of the icing. Coat the top and sides of the cake with icing. Tint the remainder with a little more colouring to give a deeper colour. Spoon into a piping bag fitted with a fluted nozzle and pipe swirls of icing around the top edge of the cake.

Decorate with a few flowers or candles and a ribbon.

Makes one 8 or 9 inch round cake

St. Clement's Sandwich Cake

6 oz. (1½ cups) self-raising flour
1 teaspoon baking powder
4 oz. (½ cup) margarine, softened
4 oz. (½ cup) castor (superfine)
  sugar
2 large eggs
2 tablespoons (3T) orange juice
finely grated rind of 1 orange
2 oz. (⅓ cup) chocolate chips
Filling:
4 oz. (½ cup) full fat soft cream
  cheese
3 tablespoons (¼ cup) lemon curd

Thoroughly grease and flour two 7 inch sandwich tins (cake layer pans). Sift the flour and baking powder together into a bowl. Add the remaining cake ingredients and beat with a wooden spoon for 1-2 minutes until the mixture is pale and smooth. Divide evenly between the prepared tins and level the tops.

Bake just above the centre of a moderate oven, 350°F, Gas Mark 4 for 25-35 minutes or until the cakes have shrunk slightly from the edge of the tins and are springy to the touch. Turn out and cool on a wire rack.

To make the filling, beat the cream cheese with the lemon curd until smooth. Sandwich the cake layers together with the lemon cheese filling.

Makes one 7 inch round cake

SIMPLE CELEBRATION CAKE

Chocolate and Mint Chequer Cake

6 oz. (¾ cup) margarine, softened
6 oz. (¾ cup) castor (superfine)
  sugar
3 large eggs
6 oz. (1½ cups) self-raising flour
1½ teaspoons baking powder
1 tablespoon cocoa powder
2 tablespoons (3T) warm water
few drops of green colouring
2-3 drops peppermint essence
  (extract)
2 tablespoons (3T) clear honey

Icing and decoration:
4 oz. (½ cup) soft margarine
9 oz. (2 cups) icing (confectioners')
  sugar, sifted
2 tablespoons (3T) hot water
  (approximately)
1 tablespoon cocoa powder
2-3 drops peppermint essence
  (extract)
few drops of green colouring
chocolate vermicelli

Grease and flour two 7 inch sandwich tins (cake layer pans). Beat together the margarine, sugar, eggs, flour and baking powder for 1-2 minutes until the mixture is pale and fluffy.

Divide the mixture in half. Blend the cocoa and water together and stir into one portion of the mixture. Spoon into one of the prepared tins. Add the green colouring and peppermint essence to the remaining mixture. Blend thoroughly. Place the mixture in the other cake tin. Smooth the tops.

Bake just above the centre of a moderate oven, 350°F, Gas Mark 4 for 25-35 minutes or until the cakes have slightly shrunk from the edges of the tins and are springy to the touch. Leave in the tins for 5 minutes before turning out. Cool on a wire rack. Place the cakes on a wooden board and cut each one into 3 rings using 1 inch and 4 inch plain cutters. Brush the cut surfaces with honey. Replace the middle chocolate ring with the peppermint ring and vice versa.

To make the icing, beat together the margarine, icing sugar and 1 tablespoon hot water. Divide the icing into 2 equal portions. Add the cocoa to one half with enough warm water to give a piping consistency. Blend thoroughly. Stir the peppermint essence and green colouring into the remaining icing.

Sandwich the cakes together with peppermint cream. Spread chocolate cream around the sides of the cake and roll in chocolate vermicelli. Decorate the top of the cake with the remaining icing.
Makes one 7 inch round cake

Fruit and Nut Crumble Cake

6 oz. (1½ cups) plain (all-purpose)
  flour
pinch of salt
½ teaspoon bicarbonate of soda
  (baking soda)
½ teaspoon ground nutmeg
3 oz. (⅓ cup) margarine, softened
3 oz. (½ cup) soft (light) brown
  sugar
¼ pint (⅔ cup) milk

1 tablespoon malt vinegar
3 oz. (½ cup) mixed dried fruit
2 oz. (½ cup) walnuts, chopped
Topping:
2 oz. (½ cup) plain (all-purpose)
  flour, sifted
2 oz. (¼ cup) castor (superfine)
  sugar
2 oz. (¼ cup) butter

Line a 6 inch round cake tin with greased greaseproof paper or non-stick parchment. Sift the flour, salt, bicarbonate of soda and nutmeg into a bowl. Add the rest of the cake ingredients and beat with a wooden spoon for 2-3 minutes until the mixture is pale and smooth.

Turn into the prepared tin and make a slight hollow in the centre. Bake at 350°F, Gas Mark 4 for 1 hour or until the cake is well-risen and firm. If the cake seems to be browning too quickly during cooking, cover with foil.

To make the topping, combine the flour and sugar and rub in the butter. Sprinkle over the cake and return to the oven for a further 30 minutes or until the topping is crisp.

Makes one 6 inch round cake

Cinnamon Apple Cake

5 oz. (⅔ cup) margarine, softened
6 oz. (¾ cup) castor (superfine)
  sugar
2 eggs
8 oz. (1¼ cups) stoned (pitted)
  dates
½ pint (1¼ cups) unsweetened
  apple purée (applesauce)
8 oz. (2 cups) wholemeal
  (wholewheat) flour

1 teaspoon baking powder
1½ teaspoons ground cinnamon
1 teaspoon mixed spice
1 teaspoon grated nutmeg
Decoration:
2 dessert apples, cored and sliced
2 tablespoons (3T) apricot jam,
  sieved

Line a 7 inch square cake tin with greased greaseproof paper or non-stick parchment. Place all the cake ingredients in a bowl and mix thoroughly. Beat for 1 minute.

Turn into the prepared tin and bake in the centre of a moderate oven, 350°F, Gas Mark 4 for about 1¼-1½ hours or until a skewer inserted into the centre of the cake comes out clean. Leave in the tin for 10 minutes before turning out onto a wire rack to cool.

Arrange the apple slices on top of the cake and brush with sieved jam to glaze.

Makes one 7 inch square cake

Quick Lemon Cake

9 oz. (2¼ cups) plain (all-purpose)
  flour
1 teaspoon baking powder
pinch of salt
6 oz. (¾ cup) margarine, softened
8 oz. (1 cup) castor (superfine)
  sugar

finely grated rind of 1 lemon
3 eggs
Filling and topping:
4-6 tablespoons (¼-½ cup) lemon
  curd
2 oz. (½ cup) icing (confectioners')
  sugar, sifted

Line a 7 or 8 inch square cake tin with greased greaseproof paper or
non-stick parchment. Sift together the flour, baking powder and salt. Add
remaining cake ingredients and beat together with a wooden spoon for
1-2 minutes until pale and smooth. Turn mixture into the prepared tin.

Bake in the centre of a cool oven, 300°F, Gas Mark 2 for 1¼-1½ hours
or until the cake is springy to the touch. Turn out and cool on a wire rack.
Split into 3 layers.

Sandwich the cake layers together with lemon curd. Dust the top
liberally with icing sugar.
Makes one 7 or 8 inch square cake

Apple and Banana Slices

4 oz. (1 cup) self-raising flour
1 teaspoon ground cinnamon
2 oz. (¼ cup) margarine, softened
4 oz. (⅔ cup) soft (light) brown
  sugar
1 egg, beaten
1 banana, mashed
1 large cooking apple, peeled,
  cored and cooked to a purée
1 oz. (¼ cup) walnuts, chopped

Icing and decoration:
4 oz. (1 cup) icing (confectioners')
  sugar
½ teaspoon ground cinnamon
2 oz. (¼ cup) soft margarine
few drops of vanilla essence
  (extract)
8 walnut halves

Line an 8 inch round cake tin with greased greaseproof paper or non-stick
parchment. Sift the flour and cinnamon together into a bowl. Add the
remaining cake ingredients and beat with a wooden spoon for
1-2 minutes. Turn into the prepared tin and smooth the top.

Bake in the centre of a moderate oven, 350°F, Gas Mark 4 for 35-45
minutes or until firm and golden brown. Turn out and cool on a wire rack.
Cut into 8 wedges.

To make the icing, sift the icing sugar and cinnamon together into a
bowl. Beat in the margarine and vanilla essence. Spoon into an icing bag
fitted with a fluted nozzle. Pipe a star border around each triangular wedge
and one star in the centre. Place a walnut on each centre star.
Makes 8 slices

QUICK LEMON CAKE *(Photograph: Kraft Foods Ltd.)*

Topaz Ring

4 oz. (1 cup) self-raising flour
1 teaspoon baking powder
4 oz. (½ cup) margarine, softened
4 oz. (½ cup) castor (superfine)
 sugar
2 eggs, beaten
finely grated rind of 1 lemon
Icing:
10 oz. (2¼ cups) icing
 (confectioners') sugar, sifted

4 oz. (½ cup) margarine, softened
1½ teaspoons black treacle
 (molasses)
1½ tablespoons (2T) lemon juice
Caramel topping:
4 oz. (½ cup) castor (superfine)
 sugar
¼ pint (⅔ cup) water
few black and green grapes

Thoroughly grease and flour a 7 inch ring mould. Sift the flour and baking powder into a bowl and add the rest of the cake ingredients. Beat for 1-2 minutes until the mixture is pale and soft.

Turn into the prepared tin and bake in the centre of a moderate oven, 350°F, Gas Mark 4 for 25-30 minutes or until the cake is springy to the touch and slightly shrunk from edges of the tin. Leave in the tin for 5 minutes before turning out onto a wire rack to cool. Cut the cake into 2 layers.

To make the icing, cream the icing sugar and margarine together until light and fluffy. Blend the treacle with 3 tablespoons (¼ cup) of the icing and sandwich the cake together with this mixture. Add the lemon juice to the remaining icing and mix thoroughly. Spread the lemon icing over the cake and using the tip of a palette knife peak up the icing.

To make the caramel, dissolve the sugar in the water over low heat. Bring to the boil and boil until the syrup turns golden brown. Remove from the heat. Carefully dip grapes into the hot caramel and then immediately into cold water. Drain thoroughly. Pour the remaining caramel onto a piece of greased greaseproof paper or non-stick parchment. When cold break into ½ inch pieces and arrange on top of the cake. Pile caramel coated grapes in the centre of the ring.

Makes one 7 inch ring cake

Lime Feather Sponge

4 oz. (1 cup) self-raising flour
1 teaspoon baking powder
4 oz. (½ cup) castor (superfine)
  sugar
4 oz. (½ cup) margarine, softened
2 large eggs
finely grated rind of 2 limes
juice of 1 lime

Filling:
3 tablespoons (¼ cup) lime
  marmalade
Icing:
4 oz. (1 cup) icing (confectioners')
  sugar
juice of 1 lime
few drops of green food colouring

Thoroughly grease and flour two 6 or 7 inch sandwich tins (cake layer pans). Sift the flour and baking powder together into a bowl. Add the rest of the cake ingredients and beat for 1-2 minutes until the mixture is pale and smooth.

Divide the mixture evenly between the prepared tins and smooth the tops. Bake just above the centre of a moderate oven, 350°F, Gas Mark 4 for 25-35 minutes or until the cakes are golden and springy to the touch. Turn out onto a wire rack to cool. Sandwich together with marmalade.

To make the icing, sift the icing sugar into a bowl. Beat in the lime juice, gradually, adding just enough to give a smooth, spreading consistency, icing. Colour 2 tablespoons (3T) of the icing with green colouring. Place in a piping bag fitted with a fine plain writing tube.

Spread the white icing over the top of the cake. Immediately pipe concentric circles of green icing, about ½ inch apart, on top. Before the icing sets, draw lines with a skewer from the centre of the cake to the edge, to divide the cake into four sections. Then draw lines from the edge of the cake to the centre between the sections to create a feathered design. Leave to set.

Makes one 6 or 7 inch round cake

Dundee Cake

8 oz. (2 cups) plain (all-purpose)
 flour
½ teaspoon baking powder
1½ teaspoons mixed spice
8 oz. (1 cup) margarine, softened
8 oz. (1 cup) castor (superfine)
 sugar
grated rind of 1 orange
4 eggs, beaten
4 oz. (⅔ cup) seedless raisins

4 oz. (⅔ cup) sultanas (seedless
 white raisins)
4 oz. (⅔ cup) currants
2 oz. (⅓ cup) mixed (candied)
 peel
3 oz. (⅓ cup) glacé (candied)
 cherries
2 oz. (½ cup) blanched almonds,
 split

Line an 8 inch round cake tin with greased greaseproof paper or non-stick parchment. Sift the flour with the baking powder and mixed spice into a mixing bowl. Add all the remaining ingredients, except the blanched almonds, and beat thoroughly with a wooden spoon for 2-3 minutes until thoroughly mixed.

Place the mixture in the prepared cake tin and level the surface. Arrange the split almonds in circles on top. Bake in a moderate oven, 325°F, Gas Mark 3 for 2¼-2½ hours or until a skewer, inserted into the centre of the cake, comes out clean.

Leave in the tin for 10 minutes then turn out and cool on a wire rack.
Makes one 8 inch round cake

Quick Marmalade Cake

4 oz. (1 cup) self-raising flour,
 sifted
4 oz. (½ cup) margarine, softened
4 oz. (½ cup) castor (superfine)
 sugar
2 large eggs

5 tablespoons (6T) chunky
 marmalade
Icing:
4 oz. (1 cup) icing (confectioners')
 sugar, sifted
1-2 tablespoons hot water

Line an 8 inch round cake tin with greased greaseproof paper or non-stick parchment. Place the flour, margarine, sugar, eggs and 3 tablespoons (¼ cup) marmalade in a bowl and beat together for 1-2 minutes until the mixture is pale and soft. Turn into the prepared tin and smooth the top.

Bake just above the centre of a moderate oven, 350°F, Gas Mark 4 for 35-40 minutes or until the cake has slightly shrunk from the edge of the tin and is springy to the touch. Leave in the tin for 5 minutes then turn out and cool on a wire rack. Spread the remaining marmalade over the cake.

To prepare the icing, gradually beat the water into the icing sugar until a thick pouring consistency is obtained. Spread the icing over the cake and leave to set.
Makes one 8 inch round cake

Lemon and Ginger Cake

10 oz. (2½ cups) wholemeal
  (wholewheat) flour
2 teaspoons baking powder
2 teaspoons ground ginger
4 oz. (½ cup) margarine, softened
4 oz. (⅔ cup) soft (light) brown
  sugar
4 oz. (⅓ cup) golden (maple)
  syrup
5 oz. (7T) black treacle (molasses)
1 large egg
⅓ pint (1 cup) milk
2 oz. (¼ cup) preserved ginger,
  chopped

Icing and decoration:
2½ oz. (¼ cup + 1T) soft
  margarine
6 oz. (1⅓ cups) icing
  (confectioners') sugar, sifted
finely grated rind of 1 lemon
1½ tablespoons (2T) lemon juice
3 oz. (¾ cup) slivered almonds,
  browned
2 tablespoons (3T) chopped
  preserved ginger
6 crystallized lemon slices, halved

Line an 8 inch square cake tin with greased greaseproof paper or non-stick parchment. Sift the flour, baking powder and ginger into a bowl. Add the rest of the cake ingredients and beat for 2-3 minutes until the mixture is pale and smooth. Pour into the prepared tin and bake in the centre of a cool oven, 300°F, Gas Mark 2 for 1½-1¾ hours or until the cake is springy to the touch. Allow to cool in the tin then remove and peel off the paper. Slice through the centre to give 2 cake layers.

To make the icing, beat together the margarine, icing sugar, lemon rind and juice. Sandwich the cake together with some of the icing. Coat the sides with icing and press on the almonds. Place on a serving plate. Spread icing over the top and pipe rosettes around the edges. Decorate with ginger and lemon slices.

Makes one 8 inch square cake

Banana Cake

10 oz. (2½ cups) self-raising flour,
  sifted
2 oz. (¼ cup) margarine, softened
4 oz. (½ cup) castor (superfine)
  sugar

1 egg
6 tablespoons (½ cup) milk
finely grated rind of 1 orange
2 oz. (½ cup) walnuts, chopped
3 bananas, mashed

Line a 2 lb. loaf tin with greased greaseproof paper or non-stick parchment. Place all ingredients in a bowl and beat for 1-2 minutes until the mixture is pale and smooth. Turn into the prepared tin and bake at 350°F, Gas Mark 4 for 1¼-1½ hours or until a skewer inserted into the centre of the cake comes out clean.

Leave in the tin for 5 minutes before turning out onto a wire rack to cool.

Makes one 2 lb. loaf cake

Chocolate Meringue Gâteau

3 oz. (¾ cup) plain (all-purpose)
  flour
1 teaspoon baking powder
1 oz. (¼ cup) cocoa powder
2 egg yolks
4 oz. (½ cup) margarine, softened
4 oz. (½ cup) castor (superfine)
  sugar
2 tablespoons (3T) water

Meringue:
4 oz. (1 cup) icing (confectioners')
  sugar, sifted
½ teaspoon cocoa powder
2 egg whites
Icing:
½ oz. (2T) cocoa powder
4 oz. (½ cup) butter
8 oz. (1¾ cups) icing
  (confectioners') sugar

Line an 8 inch round loose-bottomed cake tin with greased greaseproof paper or non-stick parchment. Sift the flour, baking powder and cocoa into a bowl. Add the rest of the cake ingredients and beat with a wooden spoon for 2-3 minutes until the mixture is smooth.

Spoon the mixture into the prepared tin and level the surface. Bake in the centre of a moderate oven, 350°F, Gas Mark 4 for 35-40 minutes or until the cake is springy to the touch. Turn out and cool on a wire rack. Cut the cake into 2 layers.

Place the meringue ingredients in a bowl over a pan of hot water and whisk until the mixture is stiff and stands in peaks. Place the meringue in a forcing bag fitted with a large fluted nozzle. Pipe small meringue stars onto baking sheets lined with greased greaseproof paper or non-stick parchment. Bake in a cool oven, 300°F, Gas Mark 2 for 30-40 minutes or until crisp. Cool on a wire rack.

To make the icing, dissolve the cocoa powder in 3 tablespoons (¼ cup) hot water. Cool. Beat the cocoa, butter and icing sugar together until soft. Sandwich the cake together with half of the icing. Spread the remaining icing over the top and sides of the cake. Decorate with the meringue.

Makes one 8 inch round gâteau

CREAMED CAKES

Cakes prepared by the creaming method require a softened fat. Butter will give a richer flavour than margarine but both are suitable. It is preferable to have all ingredients at room temperature before mixing. If necessary, creamed cake mixtures may be stored in the refrigerator overnight before baking.

Orange Layer Cake

6 oz. (¾ cup) butter
6 oz. (¾ cup) castor (superfine)
  sugar
3 large eggs, beaten
6 oz. (1½ cups) self-raising flour,
  sifted
finely grated rind of 1 orange
Icing and decoration:
8 oz. (1 cup) butter
14 oz. (3 cups) icing
  (confectioners') sugar, sifted

grated rind of 1 orange
1 tablespoon honey
few drops of orange food
  colouring
2 oranges, peeled, segmented and
  chopped
2 oz. (2 cups) cornflakes, toasted
8 crystallized orange slices, halved

Line two 8 inch sandwich tins (cake layer pans) with greased greaseproof paper or non-stick parchment. Cream the butter and sugar together until pale and fluffy. Gradually beat in the eggs. Fold in the flour and orange rind, using a metal tablespoon. Divide the mixture evenly between the prepared tins and smooth the tops.

Bake just above the centre of a moderate oven, 350°F, Gas Mark 4 for 30-40 minutes or until well-risen and springy to the touch. Turn out onto a wire rack to cool. Slice each cake in half to give 4 layers.

To make the icing, cream together the butter, icing sugar, orange rind, honey and orange food colouring until smooth and soft. Sandwich the cake layers together with some of the icing and chopped oranges. Spread the sides with icing and roll in the cornflakes. Place on a serving plate. Spread icing over the top of the cake and decorate with crystallized orange slices.

Makes one 8 inch round cake

ORANGE LAYER CAKE *(Photograph: Tate and Lyle)*

Frosted Cake

6 oz. (¾ cup) castor (superfine) sugar
6 oz. (¾ cup) butter, softened
3 eggs, beaten
6 oz. (1½ cups) self-raising flour, sifted
Filling:
1½ oz. (3T) margarine
1½ tablespoons (2T) milk
1 tablespoon brown sugar

6 oz. (1⅓ cups) icing (confectioners') sugar, sifted
Frosting and decoration:
1 lb. (3½ cups) icing (confectioners') sugar, sifted
1 egg white
juice of ½ lemon
4 tablespoons (⅓ cup) boiling water
8 walnut halves to decorate

Thoroughly grease and flour two 7 or 8 inch sandwich tins (cake layer pans). Cream together the sugar and butter until pale and fluffy. Gradually beat in the eggs. Fold in the flour, using a metal tablespoon. Turn into the prepared tins and smooth the tops.

Bake just above the centre of a moderate oven, 350°F, Gas Mark 4 for 30-40 minutes or until slightly shrunk from the edge of the tins and springy to the touch. Cool on a wire rack.

Mix all filling ingredients together in a bowl over a pan of hot water. Beat until thoroughly blended. Leave until cool. Whisk the frosting ingredients together in a bowl until the mixture stands in peaks.

Sandwich the cakes together with the filling and a layer of frosting. Spread the remaining frosting over the cake. Decorate with walnut halves.
Makes one 7 or 8 inch round cake

Coffee Frosted Cake

4 oz. (½ cup) margarine, softened
4 oz. (½ cup) castor (superfine)
  sugar
2 eggs, beaten
4 oz. (1 cup) self-raising flour,
  sifted

Frosting:
1 tablespoon golden (maple) syrup
1 oz. (2T) margarine
3 oz. (⅓ cup) full fat cream cheese
1 tablespoon coffee essence
  (strong black coffee)
7 oz. (1 ½ cups) icing
  (confectioners') sugar, sifted

Thoroughly grease and flour two 7 inch sandwich tins (cake layer pans).
Cream together the margarine and sugar until pale and fluffy. Gradually
beat in the eggs. Fold in the flour, using a metal tablespoon. Turn into the
prepared tins.

Bake just above the centre of a moderate oven, 350°F, Gas Mark 4 for
about 30 minutes or until springy to the touch and slightly shrunk from the
edge of the tins. Turn out and cool on a wire rack.

Place the syrup, margarine, cheese and coffee essence in a pan over a
low heat until melted, stirring occasionally. Pour onto the icing sugar and
beat thoroughly until the frosting is a dark golden colour. Use a little
frosting to sandwich the cakes together. Swirl the remaining frosting over
the cake.
Makes one 7 inch round cake

Orange Bran Cake

4 oz. (½ cup) margarine, softened
4 oz. (½ cup) castor (superfine)
  sugar
2 eggs, beaten
finely grated rind of 1 orange
4 tablespoons (⅓ cup) orange
  juice
6 oz. (1 ½ cups) self-raising flour,
  sifted

2 oz. (1 cup) All-bran cereal
Icing and decoration:
4 oz. (1 cup) icing (confectioners')
  sugar, sifted
1 tablespoon boiling water
  (approximately)
4 tablespoons (⅓ cup) All-bran
  cereal

Line a 6 inch round cake tin with greased greaseproof paper or non-stick
parchment. Cream together the margarine and sugar until pale and fluffy.
Gradually beat in the eggs. Fold in the rest of the cake ingredients.

Turn into the prepared tin and bake in the centre of a moderate oven,
350°F, Gas Mark 4 for approximately 1 hour or until fairly firm and slightly
shrunk from the edge of the tin. Cool in the tin for a few minutes before
turning out onto a wire rack to cool.

Combine the icing sugar with sufficient water to give a smooth coating
consistency. Pour over the cake and decorate with a ring of bran cereal.
Makes one 6 inch round cake

Blackcurrant Feather Cake

6 oz. (¾ cup) margarine, softened
6 oz. (¾ cup) castor (superfine) sugar
3 eggs, beaten
6 oz. (1½ cups) self-raising flour, sifted
1 tablespoon blackcurrant syrup or cordial

Filling:
3 oz. (⅓ cup) margarine, softened

6 oz. (1⅓ cups) icing (confectioners') sugar, sifted
1 tablespoon blackcurrant syrup or cordial

Glacé icing:
4 oz. (1 cup) icing (confectioners') sugar, sifted
1-2 tablespoons blackcurrant syrup or cordial, warmed

Line two 7 or 8 inch sandwich tins (cake layer pans) with greased greaseproof paper or non-stick parchment. Cream together the margarine and sugar until pale and fluffy. Gradually beat in the eggs. Fold in the flour and the blackcurrant syrup, using a metal tablespoon.

Turn the mixture into the prepared tins. Bake just above the centre of a moderate oven, 350°F, Gas Mark 4 for 30-40 minutes or until well-risen and springy to the touch. Turn out and cool on a wire rack.

To make the filling, beat together the margarine, icing sugar and blackcurrant syrup until soft. Sandwich the cake layers together with the filling.

To make the glacé icing, mix a few drops of hot water with 2 tablespoons (3T) of the icing sugar to give a thin piping consistency. Place in a forcing bag fitted with a fine plain writing pipe. Blend enough blackcurrant juice with the remaining icing sugar to yield a thick coating consistency. Spread the blackcurrant icing over the top of the cake and immediately pipe on straight lines of plain icing, about ½ inch apart. Quickly draw a skewer across the lines, at right angles, at 2 inch intervals. Run the skewer in the opposite directions between the intersections to create a feathered pattern.
Makes one 7 or 8 inch round cake

Snow Queen Cake

5 oz. (⅔ cup) margarine, softened
5 oz. (⅔ cup) castor (superfine)
  sugar
3 eggs, beaten
8 oz. (2 cups) self-raising flour,
  sifted
pinch of salt
4 oz. (1⅓ cups) desiccated
  (shredded) coconut
3 tablespoons (¼ cup) milk

Icing and decoration:
2 oz. (¼ cup) butter, softened
6 oz. (1⅓ cups) icing
  (confectioners') sugar
1 tablespoon milk
2 oz. (⅔ cup) desiccated
  (shredded) coconut

Line a 7 inch round cake tin with greased greaseproof paper or non-stick parchment. Cream together the margarine and sugar until pale and fluffy. Gradually beat in the eggs. Fold in the flour, salt, coconut and milk.

Turn into the prepared tin and bake in the centre of a moderate oven, 325°F, Gas Mark 3 for 1-1¼ hours or until slightly shrunk from the edge of the tin and fairly springy to the touch. Leave in the tin for 5 minutes then turn out onto a wire rack to cool.

To make the icing, beat the butter with the icing sugar and milk to give a smooth spreading consistency. Cover the top of the cake with the buttercream and sprinkle with the coconut.

Makes one 7 inch round cake

Fig and Sultana Cake

4 oz. (⅔ cup) dried figs, soaked
  overnight in cold water
4 oz. (⅔ cup) soft (light) brown
  sugar
6 oz. (¾ cup) margarine, softened
2 eggs, beaten
8 oz. (2 cups) wholemeal
  (wholewheat) flour

2 teaspoons baking powder
1 tablespoon rum
2 tablespoons (3T) milk
2 oz. (¼ cup) glacé (candied)
  cherries, chopped
2 oz. (½ cup) walnuts, chopped
4 oz. (⅔ cup) sultanas (seedless
  white raisins)

Cook the figs in their soaking liquor for 20 minutes. Drain and chop. Line a 7 inch round cake tin with greased greaseproof paper or non-stick parchment.

Cream together the sugar and margarine until pale and fluffy. Gradually beat in the eggs. Fold in the remaining ingredients, using a metal tablespoon. Turn into the prepared tin and level the surface.

Bake in the centre of a moderate oven, 325°F, Gas Mark 3 for 1½-1¾ hours or until a skewer, inserted into the centre of the cake, comes out clean. Cover with foil or greaseproof paper if the cake appears to be browning too quickly. Leave in the tin for 5 minutes before turning out onto a wire rack to cool.

Makes one 7 inch round cake

Devil's Food Cake

6 oz. (1 ½ cups) plain (all-purpose)
  flour
¼ teaspoon baking powder
1 teaspoon bicarbonate of soda
  (baking soda)
2 oz. (½ cup) cocoa powder
4 oz. (½ cup) butter, softened
10 oz. (1¼ cups) castor
  (superfine) sugar
2 eggs, beaten
8 fl. oz. (1 cup) water

Filling:
1 ½ oz. (1 ½ squares) plain
  (semi-sweet) chocolate
1 oz. (2T) butter
2 oz. (½ cup) icing (confectioners')
  sugar, sifted
Frosting:
1 lb. (2 cups) sugar
¼ pint (⅔ cup) water
2 egg whites

Line two 8 inch sandwich tins (cake layer pans) with greased greaseproof paper or non-stick parchment. Sift together the flour, baking powder, bicarbonate of soda and cocoa powder. Cream the butter and sugar together until the mixture is light and fluffy. Beat in the eggs gradually. Fold in the flour mixture and water alternately, using a metal spoon.

Divide the mixture evenly between the prepared tins and bake just above the centre of a moderate oven, 350°F, Gas Mark 4 for 50-60 minutes or until the cake is springy to the touch. Turn out and cool on a wire rack.

Melt the chocolate for the filling in a bowl over a pan of hot water. Cream the butter and icing sugar together. Gradually beat in the cooled chocolate. Sandwich the cake layers together with the chocolate icing.

To make the frosting, dissolve the sugar in the water in a large, heavy pan over low heat then raise the heat. Boil the syrup until it reaches a temperature of 240°F or until a soft ball is formed if a little syrup is dropped into cold water. Take off the heat. Whisk the egg whites until stiff. When bubbles on the syrup have subsided pour onto the egg whites in a thin steady stream, whisking all the time. Continue whisking until the frosting stiffens and holds its shape. Swirl over the cake.

Makes one 8 inch round cake

Coffee Gâteau

6 oz. (¾ cup) margarine, softened
6 oz. (¾ cup) castor (superfine)
  sugar
3 eggs, beaten
7 oz. (1¾ cups) self-raising flour,
  sifted
1½ tablespoons (2T) coffee
  essence (strong black coffee)
2 oz. (½ cup) walnuts, chopped
  (optional)

Icing and decoration:
6 oz. (¾ cup) margarine, softened
1 lb. (3½ cups) icing
  (confectioners') sugar, sifted
1-2 teaspoons coffee essence
  (strong black coffee)
1 tablespoon hot water
4 oz. (1 cup) walnut halves

Line an 8 inch round cake tin with greased greaseproof paper or non-stick parchment. Cream the margarine and sugar together until pale and fluffy. Gradually beat in the eggs. Fold in the flour, coffee essence and walnuts, if used, with a metal tablespoon. Spoon the mixture into the prepared tin and smooth the surface.

Bake in the centre of a moderate oven, 350°F, Gas Mark 4 for 35-45 minutes or until the cake is springy to the touch. Turn out onto a wire rack to cool. Cut the cake into 3 layers.

To make the coffee icing, beat together the margarine, icing sugar, coffee essence and water until smooth. Sandwich the cake layers together with some of the icing. Spread more icing over the top and sides of the cake. Press halved walnuts onto the sides of the cake. Pipe swirls of icing around the edge of the cake, topping each swirl with a walnut half.
Makes one 8 inch round cake

Variation:
Follow the above recipe, but cut the cake into 2 layers instead of 3. Sandwich together with some of the coffee icing. Decorate the top of the cake with piped swirls of the coffee icing, glacé cherries and chocolate caraque.

To make the chocolate caraque, melt 3 oz. (3 squares) plain (semi-sweet) chocolate in a bowl over hot water. Spread the melted chocolate thinly on a laminated surface. Leave until almost set then, using the edge of a palette knife, shave off pieces of chocolate to form flakes. Arrange on top of cake.

This variation is illustrated on the jacket.

Rich Fruit Cake

Suitable for Christmas, birthdays, weddings and other special occasions

12 oz. (3 cups) plain (all-purpose) flour
½ teaspoon ground cinnamon
½ teaspoon grated nutmeg
½ teaspoon mixed spice
1 lb. (2⅔ cups) currants
8 oz. (1⅓ cups) sultanas (seedless white raisins)
4 oz. (⅔ cup) seedless raisins
4 oz. (⅔ cup) prunes, chopped
2 oz. (¼ cup) glacé (candied) cherries, chopped

2 oz. (⅓ cup) mixed (candied) peel
2 tablespoons (3T) milk
5 tablespoons (6T) brandy or sherry
8 oz. (1 cup) butter, softened
8 oz. (1⅓ cups) soft (light) brown sugar
1 tablespoon black treacle (molasses)
5 large eggs, beaten

Lightly grease an 8 inch square or 9 inch round cake tin. Line with a double layer of greased greaseproof paper or non-stick parchment. Tie a double thickness of brown paper around the outside of the tin so that it comes well above the rim.

Sift together the flour, cinnamon, nutmeg and mixed spice. Place the fruit and peel in a bowl and sprinkle with the milk and 2 tablespoons (3T) of the brandy or sherry.

In a separate bowl, cream the butter with the sugar until light and fluffy. Stir in the treacle. Beat in the eggs, a little at a time, adding 1 tablespoon of flour between each addition. Fold in the flour and fruit mixture. Spoon into the prepared tin and level the surface then make a slight hollow in the centre.

Bake just below the centre of a moderate oven, 325°F, Gas Mark 3 for 1 hour. Reduce the temperature to 275°F, Gas Mark 1 and bake for a further 2-3 hours or until a skewer, inserted into the centre of the cake, comes out clean. Leave in the tin to cool slightly before turning out onto a wire rack. When completely cold, wrap in foil, seal tightly and store until a few weeks before required.

Make holes in the base of the cake and, using a small funnel, pour in 3 tablespoons (¼ cup) brandy. Reseal the cake. One week before the cake is required, cover with almond paste. Leave to harden then cover with royal icing and decorate to suit the occasion.

Makes one 8 inch square or 9 inch round cake

Note: For a two-tier wedding cake, double the above quantities and place the mixture in two round tins, 8 inches and 10 inches in diameter, or two square tins, 7 inches and 9 inches across. The depth of cake mixture should be similar in both tins. Bake as above but test the smaller cake after 2½ hours and, if necessary, at 15 minute intervals thereafter.

Almond Paste

These quantities make 2 lb. almond paste which is sufficient to cover the top and sides of an 8 inch square or 9 inch round cake. Use half quantities if the top only is to be covered. Double the quantities to cover a two-tier, 8 and 10 inch round, or 7 and 9 inch square, wedding cake.

1 lb. (4 cups) ground almonds
8 oz. (1 cup) castor (superfine)
 sugar
8 oz. (1¾ cups) icing
 (confectioners') sugar, sifted

1½ teaspoons lemon juice
few drops of almond essence
 (extract)
1 egg + 1 yolk, beaten
 (approximately)

Place the ground almonds and sugars in a bowl. Add the lemon juice and almond essence and sufficient beaten egg to give a stiff dough. Work the ingredients together with the fingers then turn onto a board, dusted with icing sugar, and knead until smooth.

To cover a cake with almond paste:
Brush top and sides of cake with warmed, sieved apricot jam. Roll out one-third of the almond paste to a round or square large enough to cover top of cake. Place on cake. Roll out remaining almond paste in a long strip to cover the sides of the cake. Apply to the sides and smooth the edges together.

Cover with a sheet of greaseproof (waxed) paper and leave in a cool place for 4 days or until the almond paste is dry and firm.

Royal Icing

3 egg whites, lightly beaten
1½-1¾ lb. (5¼-6¼ cups) icing
 (confectioners') sugar, sifted

1½ teaspoons lemon juice
2 teaspoons glycerine

Place the egg whites in a bowl. Stir in half the icing sugar then beat for 5-10 minutes until the icing is smooth, glossy and white. Beat in the lemon juice and glycerine. Continue adding more icing sugar until the icing is stiff enough to form peaks.

To cover cake with icing:
Place cake on a cake board, securing the base with a little icing. Spread three-quarters of the icing over top and sides of cake, smoothing with a palette knife. Cover the remaining icing with a dampened cloth and leave in a cool place.

Allow the cake to dry for 24 hours then decorate, as liked, with the remaining icing.

To cover Christmas cake with peaked icing:
Spread the royal icing thickly over the cake. Using a palette knife, flick the icing up to form peaks to resemble snow.

Chocolate Iced Sandwich Cake

4 oz. (½ cup) margarine, softened
4 oz. (½ cup) castor (superfine)
  sugar
2 eggs, beaten
4 oz. (1 cup) self-raising flour,
  sifted

Icing:
4 oz. (⅔ cup) plain (semi-sweet)
  chocolate chips
2 oz. (¼ cup) margarine, softened
1 egg, beaten
6 oz. (1⅓ cups) icing
  (confectioners') sugar, sifted

Thoroughly grease and flour two 7 inch sandwich tins (cake layer pans). Cream the margarine and sugar together until pale and fluffy. Gradually beat in the eggs. Fold in the flour, using a metal tablespoon. Divide the mixture evenly between the prepared tins. Smooth the tops.

Bake above the centre of a moderate oven, 350°F, Gas Mark 4 for about 30 minutes or until springy to the touch and slightly shrunk from the edge of tins. Turn out onto a wire rack to cool.

Melt the chocolate for the icing in a bowl over a pan of hot water. Add the margarine and stir until melted. Remove from the heat. Beat in the egg and icing sugar. Sandwich the layers together with icing and swirl the remainder over the top and sides of the cake.

Makes one 7 inch round cake

Iced Marble Cake

6 oz. (¾ cup) margarine, softened
6 oz. (¾ cup) castor (superfine)
  sugar
3 eggs, beaten
8 oz. (2 cups) self-raising flour,
  sifted
1 oz. (¼ cup) cocoa powder, sifted
2 tablespoons (3T) warm water

Icing:
1 tablespoon cocoa powder, sifted
1-2 tablespoons hot water
few drops of vanilla essence
  (extract)
½ oz. (1T) butter, melted
6 oz. (1⅓ cups) icing
  (confectioners') sugar, sifted

Line an 8 inch round cake tin with greased greaseproof paper or non-stick parchment. Cream the margarine and sugar together until pale and fluffy. Gradually beat in the eggs. Fold in the flour, using a metal tablespoon.

Dissolve the cocoa powder in the water and stir into half of the cake mixture. Put alternate spoonfuls of plain and chocolate mixture into the prepared tin to create a marbled effect.

Bake in the centre of a moderate oven, 325°F, Gas Mark 3 for 1-1¼ hours or until springy to the touch and slightly shrunk from the edge of the tin. Turn out and cool on a wire rack.

To make the icing, dissolve the cocoa powder in 1 tablespoon hot water. Stir in the vanilla essence and melted butter. Gradually beat in the icing sugar. Add more water, if necessary, to give a smooth coating consistency. Spread over the cake and leave to set.

Makes one 8 inch round cake

CHOCOLATE ICED SANDWICH CAKE *(Photograph: Cadbury Typhoo Food Advisory Service)*

Sachertorte

8 oz. (8 squares) plain
  (semi-sweet) chocolate
4 oz. (½ cup) unsalted (sweet)
  butter
6 oz. (¾ cup) castor (superfine)
  sugar
5 eggs, separated
3 oz. (¾ cups) hazelnuts (filberts),
  ground

1½ oz. (⅓ cup) self-raising flour,
  sifted
Filling and topping:
¼ pint (⅔ cup) double (heavy)
  cream, whipped
3 oz. (3 squares) plain
  (semi-sweet) chocolate
1½ oz. (3T) butter, melted
12 whole hazelnuts (filberts)

Line two 8 inch sandwich tins (cake layer pans) with greased greaseproof paper or non-stick parchment. Melt the chocolate in a basin over a pan of hot water. Cut the butter into small pieces and add to the chocolate. Stir until melted. Beat in the sugar. Gradually beat in the egg yolks.

Whisk the egg whites until stiff and gently fold into the chocolate mixture with the hazelnuts and flour. Turn into the prepared tins. Bake in the centre of a moderate oven, 350°F, Gas Mark 4 for 30-35 minutes. Turn out and cool on a wire rack.

Set aside enough cream to decorate the cake and sandwich the layers together with the remainder. Melt the chocolate for the topping in a basin over a pan of hot water and gradually beat in the butter. Leave for 20-30 minutes until cool and thick enough to coat the back of a spoon. Stand cake on a wire rack over a plate and pour the icing over the top and sides. Allow to set and decorate with piped cream rosettes and hazelnuts.
Makes one 8 inch round cake

Cherry and Chocolate Cake

3 oz. (⅓ cup) margarine, softened
4 oz. (½ cup) castor (superfine)
  sugar
2 eggs, beaten
8 oz. (2 cups) self-raising flour,
  sifted

2 oz. (¼ cup) glacé (candied)
  cherries, chopped
2 oz. (⅓ cup) plain (semi-sweet)
  chocolate chips
4 tablespoons (⅓ cup) milk

Line a 7 inch round cake tin with greased greaseproof paper or non-stick parchment. Cream together the margarine and sugar until pale and fluffy. Gradually beat in the eggs. Fold in the remaining ingredients, using a metal tablespoon. Turn into the prepared tin and level the surface.

Bake in the centre of a moderate oven, 350°F, Gas Mark 4 for about 1 hour or until a skewer, inserted into the centre of the cake, comes out clean. Leave in the tin for 5 minutes before turning out onto a wire rack to cool.
Makes one 7 inch round cake

Chocolate Banana Cake

6 oz. (¾ cup) margarine, softened
6 oz. (¾ cup) castor (superfine)
  sugar
3 large eggs
8 oz. (2 cups) self-raising flour,
  sifted
2 ripe bananas, mashed
Filling:
6 oz. (1 ⅓ cups) icing
  (confectioners') sugar, sifted

3 oz. (⅓ cup) butter, softened
½ oz. (2T) cocoa powder
1 tablespoon hot water
Glacé icing and decoration:
6 oz. (1 ⅓ cups) icing
  (confectioners') sugar
1 tablespoon cocoa powder
1-2 tablespoons hot water
12 chocolate buttons

Line two 8 inch sandwich tins (cake layer pans) with greased greaseproof paper or non-stick parchment. Cream the margarine and sugar together until light and fluffy. Beat in the eggs, one at a time. Fold in the flour and bananas, using a metal tablespoon.

Divide the mixture evenly between the prepared tins and bake just above the centre of a moderate oven, 350°F, Gas Mark 4 for 30-40 minutes until springy to the touch. Turn out and cool on a wire rack.

Place the icing sugar and butter in a bowl and work together using a fork. Blend the cocoa powder with the water and add to the creamed mixture. Beat until light and smooth. Sandwich the cake together with the filling.

To make the glacé icing, sift the icing sugar and cocoa powder into a bowl. Blend with enough hot water to give a smooth spreading icing. Spread over top of cake and arrange chocolate buttons around edge.
Makes one 8 inch round cake

Spicy Chocolate Cake

3 oz. (3 squares) plain
  (semi-sweet) chocolate
4 oz. (½ cup) margarine, softened
6 oz. (¾ cup) castor (superfine)
  sugar
2 eggs, separated

½ teaspoon ground cinnamon
½ teaspoon mixed spice
6 oz. (1 ½ cups) self-raising flour,
  sifted
¼ pint (⅔ cup) milk

Line a 7 inch square cake tin with greased greaseproof paper or non-stick parchment. Melt the chocolate in a bowl over a pan of hot water. Cream together the margarine and sugar until pale and fluffy. Blend in the melted chocolate and egg yolks. Fold in the spices, flour and milk, using a metal spoon. Whisk the egg whites until stiff then fold into the mixture.

Bake immediately in the centre of a moderate oven, 350°F, Gas Mark 4 for about 1 hour or until slightly shrunk from the sides of the tin and springy to the touch. Turn out and cool on a wire rack. Serve plain or spread with a chocolate topping as for Sachertorte (page 46).
Makes one 7 inch square cake

Rich Chocolate Layer Cake

3 oz. (¾ cup) cocoa powder
6 tablespoons (½ cup) boiling
  water
11 oz. (1 ⅝ cups) castor
  (superfine) sugar
6 fl. oz. (¾ cup) milk
8 oz. (1 cup) butter, softened
4 eggs, separated
8 oz. (2 cups) self-raising flour
1 teaspoon baking powder

Filling:
¼ pint (⅔ cup) double (heavy)
  cream
¼ pint (⅔ cup) single (light) cream
Topping:
icing (confectioners') sugar for
  dusting

Blend the cocoa with the boiling water in a small bowl. Add 3 oz. (⅓ cup) of the sugar and mix to a smooth paste. Place the bowl over a pan of hot water and cook until the mixture is thick and shiny. Stir in the milk and leave to cool.

Cream the butter with the remaining sugar until the mixture is light and fluffy. Beat in the egg yolks together with the chocolate mixture. Sift together the flour and baking powder and fold into the mixture, using a metal spoon. Whisk the egg whites until stiff then carefully fold into the mixture.

Line two 8 inch sandwich tins (cake layer pans) with greased greaseproof paper or non-stick parchment. Divide the cake mixture evenly between the tins. Bake just above the centre of a moderate oven, 350°F, Gas Mark 4 for about 40 minutes or until the cakes are springy to the touch when gently pressed. Remove from the oven but leave in the tins for 5 minutes before turning out. Remove the paper and cool on a wire rack.

Whisk the double (heavy) cream and single (light) cream together until thick. Split each cake into 2 layers. Use the cream to sandwich the 4 layers together. Just before serving, sprinkle with icing sugar.
Makes one 8 inch round cake

Jewel Cake

10 oz. (2½ cups) plain
  (all-purpose) flour
1 teaspoon ground cinnamon
1 teaspoon mixed spice
10 oz. (1¼ cups) butter
10 oz. (1¼ cups) castor
  (superfine) sugar
2 tablespoons (3T) honey
5 eggs, beaten
2 oz. (½ cup) ground almonds
finely grated rind of 1 lemon
12 oz. (2 cups) sultanas (seedless
  white raisins)
12 oz. (2 cups) seedless raisins
4 oz. (½ cup) glacé (candied)
  pineapple, chopped
4 oz. (⅔ cup) mixed (candied)
  peel, chopped

3 oz. (⅓ cup) glacé (candied)
  cherries, quartered
2 oz. (½ cup) blanched almonds,
  chopped
2 oz. (½ cup) walnuts, chopped
2 oz. (⅓ cup) dried apricots,
  chopped
1 tablespoon brandy
Icing:
1 lb. (3½ cups) icing
  (confectioners') sugar, sifted
1 egg white, lightly beaten
1 tablespoon liquid glucose
1 oz. (¼ cup) cornflour
  (cornstarch) sifted

Line an 8 inch round cake tin with greased greaseproof paper or non-stick parchment. Tie a double thickness of brown paper around the outside of the tin so that it comes well above the rim.

Sift together the flour, cinnamon and mixed spice. Cream the butter, sugar and honey together until pale and fluffy. Gradually beat in the eggs, adding 1 tablespoon of the flour between each addition. Fold in all the remaining cake ingredients and turn into the prepared tin. Smooth the surface and make a slight hollow in the centre.

Bake in the centre of a moderate oven, 325°F, Gas Mark 3 for 1 hour. Reduce the heat to 300°F, Gas Mark 2 and cook for a further 1¾-2¼ hours or until a skewer, inserted into the centre of the cake, comes out clean. Cover with foil or greaseproof paper if the cake appears to be browning too quickly. Leave in the tin until quite cold.

To make the icing, knead together the icing sugar, egg white and liquid glucose until smooth. Sprinkle a laminated surface or wooden board with the cornflour and roll out the icing to a round large enough to cover the top and sides of the cake. Mould the icing around the cake and decorate as liked.

Makes one 8 inch round cake

White Christmas Cake

9 oz. (1 cup + 2T) butter, softened
9 oz. (1 cup + 2T) castor (superfine) sugar
4 large eggs, beaten
12 oz (3 cups) plain (all-purpose) flour
4 oz (½ cup) glacé (candied) cherries, washed, dried and chopped
4 oz. (½ cup) glacé (candied) pineapple, chopped
4 oz. (1 cup) walnuts, chopped
4 oz. (⅔ cup) mixed (candied) peel, chopped
4 oz. (½ cup) preserved ginger
4 oz. (⅔ cup) sultanas (seedless white raisins)
3 tablespoons (¼ cup) brandy

Line a 7 inch square or 8 inch round cake tin with greased greaseproof paper or non-stick parchment. Cream together the butter and sugar until pale and fluffy. Gradually beat in the eggs, adding a little of the flour with each addition. Fold in the rest of the ingredients. Turn into prepared tin.

Bake in the centre of a moderate oven, 325°F, Gas Mark 3 for about 1½ hours or until a skewer, inserted into the centre of the cake, comes out clean. Cool in tin.

If desired, cover with almond paste and royal icing (page 43).
Makes one 7 inch square or 8 inch round cake

Fruity Beer Cake

4 oz. (½ cup) butter, softened
4 oz. (⅔ cup) soft (light) brown sugar
2 eggs, beaten
5 oz. (1¼ cups) plain (all-purpose) flour, sifted
1 teaspoon mixed spice
8 oz. (1⅓ cups) sultanas (seedless white raisins)
2 oz. (4T) glacé (candied) cherries
2 oz. (½ cup) walnuts, chopped
3 tablespoons (¼ cup) stout or brown ale
Topping:
2 oz. (½ cup) flour
½ teaspoon ground cinnamon
1 oz. (2T) butter
2 oz. (⅓ cup) soft (light) brown sugar
1 oz. (2T) glacé (candied) cherries, chopped
1 oz. (¼ cup) walnuts, chopped

Line a 7 inch round cake tin with greased greaseproof paper or non-stick parchment. Cream the butter and sugar together until light and fluffy. Add the eggs gradually, beating thoroughly after each addition. Fold in the flour, mixed spice, sultanas, chopped cherries and walnuts. Stir in the stout or brown ale, to give a soft dropping consistency. Turn into the prepared tin, smooth the top and make a slight hollow in the centre.

To make the topping, combine the flour and cinnamon in a bowl. Rub in the butter then stir in the remaining ingredients. Sprinkle over cake.

Bake in the centre of a moderate oven, 350°F, Gas Mark 4 for 1-1¼ hours or until a skewer, inserted into the centre of the cake, comes out clean. Leave to cool in the tin.
Makes one 7 inch round cake

Vanilla Sandwich Cake

4 oz. (½ cup) soft margarine
4 oz. (½ cup) castor (superfine)
  sugar
2 eggs, beaten
4 oz. (1 cup) self-raising flour
few drops of vanilla essence
  (extract)
Filling:
1 teaspoon cornflour (cornstarch)

¼ pint (⅔ cup) milk
2 oz. (¼ cup) margarine, softened
2 oz. (¼ cup) sugar
few drops of vanilla essence
  (extract)
4 tablespoons (⅓ cup) jam
Topping:
1 oz. (2T) castor (superfine) sugar

Thoroughly grease and flour two 7 inch sandwich tins (cake layer pans). Cream the margarine and sugar together until the mixture is pale and fluffy. Gradually beat in the eggs. Fold in the flour and vanilla essence, using a metal tablespoon.

Divide the mixture evenly between the prepared tins and smooth the tops. Bake just above the centre of a moderate oven, 350°F, Gas Mark 4 for about 30 minutes or until springy to the touch and slightly shrunk from the edge of the tins. Turn out onto a wire rack to cool.

To make the filling, blend the cornflour with a little of the milk in a small pan. Stir in the remaining milk and bring to the boil. Cook, stirring, until the mixture has thickened. Take off the heat. Cover with a dampened sheet of greaseproof paper or non-stick parchment to prevent a skin forming and leave until quite cold.

Cream together the margarine and sugar until pale and fluffy. Gradually beat in the cold cornflour mixture and add vanilla essence to taste. Sandwich the cake layers together with the jam and vanilla filling. Sprinkle the top with sugar.

Makes one 7 inch round cake
If preferred, the vanilla filling may be substituted by fresh whipped cream.

Fruity Layer Cake

6 oz. (¾ cup) butter, softened
6 oz. (¾ cup) castor (superfine)
  sugar
3 large eggs, beaten
6 oz. (1½ cups) self-raising flour,
  sifted
6 oz. (1 cup) mixed dried fruit
finely grated rind of 1 orange
few drops of vanilla essence
  (extract)

Icing and decoration:
6 oz. (¾ cup) butter
2 tablespoons (3T) rose hip syrup
1 teaspoon mixed spice
9 oz. (2 cups) icing (confectioners')
  sugar, sifted
few drops of pink food colouring
4 oz. (1 cup) slivered almonds
few glacé (candied) cherries,
  halved

Line a 9 inch square cake tin with greased greaseproof paper or non-stick parchment. Cream together the butter and sugar until pale and fluffy. Gradually beat in the eggs. Fold in the flour, fruit, orange rind and vanilla essence, using a metal tablespoon. Turn into the prepared tin.

Bake just above the centre of a moderate oven, 350°F, Gas Mark 4 for about 40 minutes or until slightly shrunk from the sides of the tin and springy to the touch. Insert a skewer into the centre of the cake; if it comes out clean the cake is cooked. Turn out onto a wire rack to cool. Cut into 3 equal pieces.

To make the icing, blend the butter and rose hip syrup together. Add the mixed spice. Gradually beat in the icing sugar. Add a few drops of colouring to give a pale pink colour.

Sandwich the cake together with some of the icing and cover the sides and top with more icing. Press almonds to the side of the cake, reserving a few for the top. Using the remaining icing, pipe rosettes along top and lower edges of the cake. Decorate the top with halved cherries and reserved almonds.

Make one 9 × 3 inch cake

Apple Cake

½ pint (1 ¼ cups) milk
1 ½ oz. (¼ cup) semolina
4 oz. (½ cup) margarine, softened
4 oz. (½ cup) castor (superfine)
  sugar
3 eggs, separated
4 oz. (2 cups) fresh breadcrumbs

¼ teaspoon ground cinnamon
2 oz. (½ cup) almonds, blanched
  and chopped
2 oz. (⅓ cup) seedless raisins
2 dessert apples, peeled, cored
  and chopped

Grease an 8 inch round loose-bottomed cake tin. Place the milk and semolina in a saucepan over moderate heat. Bring to the boil and simmer for 2 minutes, stirring all the time. Cool.

Cream together the margarine and sugar until fluffy. Beat in the egg yolks and semolina. Fold in the breadcrumbs, cinnamon, almonds, raisins and apples. Whisk the egg whites until stiff and gently fold into the mixture, using a metal spoon. Turn into the prepared tin.

Bake in the centre of a moderate oven, 350°F, Gas Mark 4 for 1-1¼ hours or until a skewer, inserted into the centre of the cake, comes out clean. Cover with foil or greaseproof paper if the cake shows signs of browning too quickly. Leave in the tin for a few minutes before turning out onto a wire rack to cool.

Makes one 8 inch round cake

Dutch Apple Walnut Cake

6 oz. (¾ cup) unsalted (sweet)
  butter, softened
6 oz. (¾ cup) castor (superfine)
  sugar
3 eggs, beaten
juice and finely grated rind of 1
  lemon

2 dessert apples, quartered and
  cored
3 oz. (¾ cup) walnuts
6 oz. (1 ½ cups) self-raising flour,
  sifted
3 tablespoons (¼ cup) apricot
  jam, warmed and sieved

Line a 7 inch round cake tin with greased greaseproof paper or non-stick parchment. Cream the butter and sugar together until pale and fluffy. Gradually beat in the eggs, lemon juice and rind. Peel and chop one of the apple quarters. Set aside about 8 walnut halves and chop the remainder. Fold the chopped apple, chopped walnuts and flour into the mixture.

Spoon the mixture into the prepared tin and level the surface. Arrange the apple quarters and walnut halves around the edge. Bake in the centre of a moderate oven, 325°F, Gas Mark 3 for 1-1½ hours or until the cake is golden brown and springy to the touch. Leave in the tin for a few minutes before turning out onto a wire rack to cool.

Brush the top with apricot jam to glaze.

Makes one 7 inch round cake

Simnel Cake

6 oz. (¾ cup) butter, softened
6 oz (1 cup) soft (light) brown
  sugar
3 eggs, beaten
8 oz. (2 cups) plain (all-purpose)
  flour
pinch of salt
1½ teaspoons mixed spice
6 oz. (1 cup) seedless raisins

6 oz. (1 cup) sultanas (seedless
  white raisins)
4 oz. (⅔ cup) currants
3 oz. (½ cup) mixed (candied)
  peel, chopped
2 tablespoons (3T) milk
1½ lb. almond paste, see page 43
honey or apricot jam to glaze
angelica leaves to decorate

Line a 7 inch round cake tin with greased greaseproof paper or non-stick parchment. Cream the butter and sugar until pale and fluffy. Gradually beat in the eggs, adding a little of the flour with each addition. Fold in the flour, salt, spice, fruit, peel and milk. Leave in a cool place.

Divide the almond paste into 3 equal portions. Roll out one-third into a circle the size of the cake tin. Place half the cake mixture in the prepared tin and press down firmly. Lay the circle of almond paste on the raw mixture. Cover with the remaining cake mixture and level the surface. Bake in the centre of a cool oven, 300°F, Gas Mark 2 for 2¾-3 hours or until a skewer, inserted into the centre of the cake, comes out clean. Cover with a sheet of foil if the cake shows signs of browning too much. Cool in the tin.

Take another third of the almond paste and roll out to a 7 inch circle. Brush the top of the cake with honey or apricot jam and place the almond paste round on top. Flute the edge. Shape the remaining almond paste into 12 small balls. Arrange on top of the cake with the angelica leaves.
Makes one 7 inch round cake

Cherry and Almond Cake

4 oz. (½ cup) margarine, softened
4 oz. (½ cup) castor (superfine)
  sugar
2 eggs, beaten
2 oz. (¼ cup) glacé (candied)
  cherries, chopped

4 oz. (1 cup) plain (all-purpose)
  flour, sifted
2 oz. (½ cup) ground almonds
few drops of almond essence
  (extract)

Line a 6 inch round cake tin with greased greaseproof paper or non-stick parchment. Cream the margarine and sugar together until pale and fluffy. Add the eggs gradually, beating thoroughly after each addition. Toss the cherries in the flour and fold into the mixture together with the ground almonds and essence.

Turn into the prepared tin and bake in the centre of a moderate oven, 325°F, Gas Mark 3 for 1½-1¾ hours or until a skewer, inserted into the centre of the cake, comes out clean. Leave in the tin for 5 minutes before turning out onto a wire rack to cool.
Makes one 6 inch round cake

SIMNEL CAKE *(Photograph: Sultana and Raisin Producing Countries)*

Coffee Ring

4 oz. (½ cup) margarine, softened
4 oz. (½ cup) castor (superfine)
  sugar
2 eggs, beaten
4 oz. (1 cup) self-raising flour,
  sifted
1 tablespoon coffee essence
  (strong black coffee)

Filling:
1½ oz. (3T) margarine
4 oz. (1 cup) icing (confectioners')
  sugar, sifted

1 teaspoon milk
2 teaspoons coffee essence
  (strong black coffee)

Icing and decoration:
2 oz. (¼ cup) margarine
1 lb. (3½ cups) icing
  (confectioners') sugar, sifted
2 tablespoons (3T) coffee essence
  (strong black coffee)
4 tablespoons (⅓ cup) milk
10 walnut halves

Thoroughly grease and flour an 8 or 9 inch ring mould. Cream together
the margarine and sugar until pale and fluffy. Gradually beat in the eggs.
Fold in the flour and coffee essence. Turn into the prepared tin. Smooth
the top.

Bake in the centre of a moderate oven, 325°F, Gas Mark 3 for 40-50
minutes or until springy to the touch and slightly shrunk from the edges of
the tin. Turn out and cool on a wire rack. Cut into 3 layers.

Beat all filling ingredients together until smooth. Sandwich the ring
together with the coffee filling. Stand on the wire rack over a plate.

To make the icing, beat the margarine, icing sugar, coffee essence and
milk together in a bowl over a pan of hot water until smooth. Pour over the
top and sides of the cake to cover completely. Decorate with walnuts.
Leave to set.

Makes one 8 or 9 inch ring cake

Orange Marmalade Cake

6 oz. (¾ cup) butter, softened
6 oz. (¾ cup) castor (superfine)
  sugar
3 eggs, separated
10 oz. (2 ½ cups) self-raising flour,
  sifted
2 oz. (⅓ cup) chopped mixed
  (candied) peel

3 tablespoons (¼ cup) marmalade
grated rind of 1 orange
1 tablespoon orange juice
Icing and decoration:
1-2 tablespoons orange juice
4 oz. (1 cup) icing (confectioners')
  sugar, sifted
2-3 crystallized orange slices

Line a 7 inch round cake tin with greased greaseproof paper or non-stick parchment. Cream the butter and sugar together until pale and fluffy. Beat in the egg yolks with 1 tablespoon of the flour. Fold in the remaining flour, mixed peel, marmalade, orange rind and juice. Whisk the egg whites until stiff and gently fold into the mixture. Turn into the prepared tin.

Bake in the centre of a moderate oven, 350°F, Gas Mark 4 for 1-1 ¼ hours or until well-risen and firm to the touch. Leave in the tin for 10 minutes before turning out onto a wire rack to cool.

Mix sufficient orange juice with the icing sugar to give a smooth coating consistency. Stand the cake on a wire rack over a plate. Pour the icing over the top. Decorate with crystallized orange slices.

Makes one 7 inch round cake

Strawberry Meringue Gâteau

2 oz. (¼ cup) butter, softened
4 oz. (½ cup) castor (superfine)
  sugar
4 egg yolks
4 oz. (1 cup) self-raising flour,
  sifted
5 tablespoons (6T) milk
Meringue:
4 egg whites

8 oz. (1 cup) castor (superfine)
  sugar
1 tablespoon chopped almonds
Filling:
¼ pint (⅔ cup) double (heavy)
  cream, lightly whipped or 1
  packet Dream Topping made up
  with ¼ pint (⅔ cup) milk
6 oz (1 cup) strawberries, halved

Line two 9 inch sandwich tins (cake layer pans) with greased greaseproof paper or non-stick parchment. Cream the butter and sugar together until light and creamy. Gradually beat in the egg yolks. Gently fold in the flour and milk. Divide the mixture between the prepared tins. Level the tops.

Whisk the egg whites for the meringue until stiff, then gradually whisk in the sugar. Spread evenly over the cake mixture and sprinkle with almonds.

Bake in the centre of a moderate oven, 350°F, Gas Mark 4 for 35-40 minutes until the meringue is crisp. Transfer to a wire rack to cool.

Sandwich the layers together with whipped cream or Dream Topping and most of the strawberries. Decorate with the remaining strawberries.

Makes one 9 inch round gâteau

St. Valentine's Cake

3 oz. (⅓ cup) butter, softened
3 tablespoons (¼ cup) clear honey
1½ oz. (⅓ cup) chocolate powder
  (sweetened cocoa)
2 eggs, beaten
4 oz. (1 cup) self-raising flour,
  sifted
pinch of salt
2 oz. (⅓ cup) seedless raisins
2 oz. (⅓ cup) sultanas (seedless
  white raisins)

Icing and decoration:
1½ oz. (3T) margarine, softened
1 tablespoon cocoa powder, sifted
9 oz. (2 cups) icing (confectioners')
  sugar, sifted
8 dried apricots, soaked, drained
  and halved
1 tablespoon hot water
  (approximately)

Thoroughly grease a heart-shaped tin, which is 9 × 9 inches across the widest part, or an 8 inch round cake tin. Cream the butter with the honey and chocolate powder until light and fluffy. Gradually beat in the eggs. Fold in the flour, salt and fruit. Turn into the prepared tin and level the surface.

Bake in the centre of a moderate oven, 350°F, Gas Mark 4 for 40-50 minutes or until the cake is springy to the touch. Turn out and cool on a wire rack. If using a round cake tin, cut the cake into a heart-shape.

Beat the margarine, cocoa and 3 oz. (⅔ cup) icing sugar together until light and fluffy. Spread some of the icing around the sides of the cake and press on the apricot halves. Place the remaining icing in a forcing bag fitted with a fluted nozzle.

Mix the remaining icing sugar with sufficient hot water to give a smooth, coating consistency, glacé icing. Pour onto the centre of the cake and allow to spread. Pipe chocolate stars around the edges of the cake.

Makes one Valentine's cake

OIL-BASED CAKES

Cakes made with oil are easy to prepare and have a consistency, before cooking, similar to that of a thick batter. Oil tends to yield a slightly heavier texture, so to counteract this effect extra raising agent is required. Either the egg whites are whisked before adding to the mixture or a little baking powder is added.

Lemon Sponge

4 oz. (1 cup) self-raising flour
2 oz. (½ cup) cornflour
 (cornstarch)
½ teaspoon salt
4 oz. (½ cup) castor (superfine)
 sugar
finely grated rind and juice of 1
 lemon
2 large eggs, separated
5 tablespoons (6T) corn oil
3 tablespoons (¼ cup) milk

Filling:
2 tablespoons (3T) lemon curd
Icing and decoration:
4 oz. (½ cup) soft margarine
2 oz. (¼ cup) castor (superfine)
 sugar
1 tablespoon boiling water
1 tablespoon lemon curd
4 oz. (4 squares) plain
 (semi-sweet) chocolate

Line two 7 inch sandwich tins (cake layer pans) with greased greaseproof paper or non-stick parchment. Sift together the flour, cornflour and salt. Add the sugar and lemon rind. Combine the egg yolks, oil, milk and lemon juice, add to the dry ingredients and beat to form a smooth batter. Whisk the egg whites until stiff and gently fold into the mixture, using a metal tablespoon.

Pour into the prepared tins and bake above the centre of a moderately hot oven, 375°F, Gas Mark 5 for 25-30 minutes or until golden brown and springy to the touch. Allow to cool slightly in the tins before turning out onto a wire rack to cool completely. Sandwich the cake layers together with lemon curd.

To make the icing, beat together the margarine, sugar, water and lemon curd until smooth. Melt 2 oz. (2 squares) of the chocolate in a bowl over a pan of hot water. Spread the melted chocolate on a sheet of greaseproof (waxed) paper and leave until almost set. Cut out shapes using a small fluted cutter. Grate the remaining chocolate.

Spread icing around the sides of the cake and roll in grated chocolate. Cover top of cake with remaining icing and decorate with chocolate shapes.
Makes one 7 inch round cake

Crispy Chocolate Cake

8 oz. (2 cups) self-raising flour
½ teaspoon baking powder
2 oz. (½ cup) cocoa powder, sifted
½ teaspoon salt
8 oz. (1 cup) castor (superfine)
  sugar
8 fl. oz. (1 cup) milk

1 teaspoon lemon juice
¼ pint (⅔ cup) corn oil
Topping:
1 oz (2T) soft margarine
2 tablespoons (3T) honey
1 oz. (1 cup) cocoa-flavoured
  crisped rice

Line an 8 inch round cake tin with greased greaseproof paper or non-stick parchment. Sift the flour, baking powder, cocoa and salt into a bowl. Stir in the sugar. Whisk the milk, lemon juice and corn oil together then add to the dry ingredients. Beat until a smooth batter is obtained. Pour into the tin.

Bake in the centre of a moderate oven, 325°F, Gas Mark 3 for 1¼-1½ hours or until springy to the touch. Turn out and cool on a wire rack.

To make the topping, place the margarine and honey in a pan over low heat and stir until melted. Mix in the cocoa-flavoured crisped rice. Smooth topping over cake and leave in a cool place to set.

Makes one 8 inch round cake

Fudge Filled Cake

5 oz. (1¼ cups) self-raising flour,
  sifted
1 teaspoon baking powder
¼ teaspoon salt
4 oz. (½ cup) castor (superfine)
  sugar
7 tablespoons (⅓ cup) corn oil
2 tablespoons (3T) milk
2 eggs
few drops of vanilla essence
  (extract)

Filling:
4 oz. (⅔ cup) soft (light) brown
  sugar
2 oz. (¼ cup) margarine
1 teaspoon coffee essence (strong
  black coffee)
1 tablespoon golden (maple)
  syrup
1 tablespoon milk
Topping:
1 oz. (2T) castor (superfine) sugar

Line two 7 inch sandwich tins (cake layer pans) with greased greaseproof paper or non-stick parchment. Sift together the flour, baking powder and salt. Stir in the sugar. Whisk the oil, milk, eggs and vanilla essence together. Add to the dry ingredients and beat for 1-2 minutes to give a smooth batter.

Pour mixture into prepared tins. Bake just above the centre of a moderate oven, 350°F, Gas Mark 4 for 25-30 minutes or until golden brown and springy to the touch. Turn out and cool on a wire rack.

Place all the filling ingredients in a small pan and bring to the boil, stirring. Simmer for 10 minutes, stirring all the time. Remove from heat and allow to cool. Beat until thick. Sandwich the cake layers together with the filling. Sprinkle sugar on top.

Makes one 7 inch round cake

MELTING METHOD CAKES

These cakes have a fairly close texture and are generally quite moist. They should be baked as soon as the ingredients have been mixed together.

Almond Gingerbread

8 oz. (2 cups) plain (all-purpose) flour
pinch of salt
2 teaspoons ground ginger
1 teaspoon bicarbonate of soda (baking soda)
2 oz. (½ cup) ground almonds
4 oz. (½ cup) margarine

4 oz. (⅓ cup) golden (maple) syrup
4 oz. (⅔ cup) soft (light) brown sugar
5 fl. oz. (⅔ cup) natural (unflavored) yogurt
1 egg, beaten
2 oz. (½ cup) slivered almonds

Line a 7 inch square cake tin with greased greaseproof paper or non-stick parchment. Sift the flour, salt, ginger and bicarbonate of soda together into a bowl. Stir in the ground almonds.

Gently melt the margarine, syrup and sugar in a pan over low heat. Make a well in the centre of the dry ingredients and pour in the syrup mixture. Add the yogurt and egg and beat until smooth. Pour into the prepared tin. Scatter the almonds on top.

Bake in the centre of a moderate oven, 325°F, Gas Mark 3 for 55-65 minutes or until the gingerbread is well-risen and springy to the touch. Leave in the tin for 15 minutes, then turn out and cool on a wire rack.
Makes 9-12 squares

Peanut Cake

12 oz. (3 cups) self-raising flour
pinch of ground cinnamon
2 tablespoons (3T) golden (maple) syrup
3 oz. (½ cup) soft (light) brown sugar

3 oz. (⅓ cup) margarine
2 tablespoons (3T) milk
6 oz. (¾ cup) crunchy peanut butter
3 eggs, beaten

Line two 1 lb. loaf tins with greased greaseproof paper or non-stick parchment. Sift the flour and cinnamon into a bowl. Gently melt the syrup, sugar and margarine in a pan over low heat. Add the milk. Make a well in the centre of the flour. Pour in the syrup mixture. Add peanut butter and eggs. Beat until smooth.

Pour into the prepared tins and bake in a moderate oven, 325°F, Gas Mark 3 for 40-50 minutes or until a skewer, inserted into the centre, comes out clean. Cool slightly in the tins before turning out onto a wire rack.
Makes two 1 lb. loaf cakes

Plain Fruit Cake

¼ pint (⅔ cup) water
8 oz. (1⅓ cups) mixed dried fruit
2 oz. (¼ cup) margarine
2 oz. (⅓ cup) soft (light) brown
  sugar
4 oz. (1 cup) plain (all-purpose)
  flour

½ teaspoon mixed spice
½ teaspoon bicarbonate of soda
  (baking soda)
1 egg, beaten

Line a 1 lb. loaf tin with greased greaseproof paper or non-stick parchment. Place the water, dried fruit, margarine and sugar in a pan over moderate heat. Bring to the boil and simmer for 10 minutes. Leave to cool.

Sift the flour, spice and bicarbonate of soda together into a bowl. Pour in the dried fruit mixture and beaten egg. Beat thoroughly.

Turn into the prepared tin and bake in the centre of a moderate oven, 350°F, Gas Mark 4 for approximately 1 hour or until a skewer, inserted into the centre of the cake, comes out clean. If the cake appears to be browning too quickly, cover with a sheet of foil or greaseproof paper. Allow to cool in the tin.

Makes one 1 lb. loaf cake

Honey Spice Cake

2 oz. (¼ cup) butter
5 oz. (7½T) honey
5 oz. (¾ cup + 1½T) demerara
  (raw) sugar
10 oz. (2½ cups) plain
  (all-purpose) flour
1 teaspoon bicarbonate of soda
  (baking soda)
1 teaspoon baking powder

1 teaspoon mixed spice
1 teaspoon ground cinnamon
1 teaspoon ground ginger
4 oz. (¾ cup) mixed (candied)
  peel, chopped
1 egg, beaten
¼ pint (⅔ cup) milk
2 oz. (½ cup) nuts, chopped

Line one 2 lb. loaf tin or two 1 lb. loaf tins with greased greaseproof paper or non-stick parchment. Melt the butter in a pan over low heat. Stir in the honey and demerara sugar. Cool.

Sift together the flour, bicarbonate of soda, baking powder and spices into a bowl. Add the mixed peel. Beat the egg and milk together and gradually beat in the honey mixture. Make a well in the centre of the dry ingredients and pour in the syrup mixture. Beat until smooth.

Place the mixture in the prepared tin and sprinkle the chopped nuts on top. Bake in the centre of a moderate oven, 350°F, Gas Mark 4. Allow about 1 hour for 1 lb. tins and 1¼-1½ hours for 2 lb. tins. The cakes are cooked when a skewer, inserted into the centre, comes out clean. Leave in the tins for 5 minutes before turning out onto a wire rack to cool.

Makes one 2 lb. or two 1 lb. loaf cakes

Oaty Ginger Cake

5 oz. (1 ¼ cups) self-raising flour
½ teaspoon salt
1 tablespoon ground ginger
1 teaspoon ground cinnamon
5 oz. (1 ½ cups) rolled oats
6 oz. (1 cup) soft (light) brown
  sugar

6 oz. (½ cup) black treacle
  (molasses)
4 oz. (½ cup) margarine
2 eggs, beaten
½ pint (1 ¼ cups) milk
2 oz. (½ cup) walnuts, chopped
4 oz. (⅔ cup) seedless raisins

Line a 7 or 8 inch square cake tin with greased greaseproof paper or non-stick parchment. Sift the flour, salt, ginger and cinnamon together into a bowl. Add the oats and sugar.

Warm the treacle and margarine in a pan over low heat until the margarine has melted. Cool. Make a well in the centre of the dry ingredients and pour in the treacle mixture together with the beaten eggs and milk. Beat until smooth. Stir in the walnuts and raisins.

Pour into the prepared tin. Bake in the centre of a moderate oven, 325°F, Gas Mark 3 for 1-1½ hours until the cake is springy to the touch and slightly shrunk from the edges of the tin. Cover with foil or greaseproof paper if the top seems to be browning too quickly. Cool in the tin.
Makes one 7 or 8 inch square cake

Apple Gingerbread

8 oz. (2 cups) cooking apples,
  peeled and sliced
3 oz. (½ cup) demerara (raw)
  sugar
4 oz. (⅓ cup) golden (maple)
  syrup
3 oz. (⅓ cup) margarine
6 oz. (1 ½ cups) self-raising flour

1 teaspoon ground ginger
1 teaspoon ground cloves
1 egg, beaten
Icing:
6 oz. (1 ⅓ cups) icing
  (confectioners') sugar
1 teaspoon ground cinnamon
1-2 tablespoons cider, warmed

Line an 8 inch square cake tin or an 11 × 7 inch Swiss (jelly) roll tin with greased greaseproof paper or non-stick parchment. Place the apples and 1 oz. (2T) of the sugar in a pan and add 2-3 tablespoons water. Cover and simmer until the apples are tender. Sieve or liquidize to a purée.

Warm the syrup, margarine and remaining sugar in a separate pan until the margarine has melted. Cool. Sift the flour, ginger and cloves together into a bowl. Make a well in the centre of the dry ingredients and add the syrup mixture, apple purée and beaten egg. Beat thoroughly.

Pour the mixture into the prepared tin and bake above the centre of a moderate oven, 350°F, Gas Mark 4 for 30-40 minutes or until well-risen and springy to the touch. Cool in the tin.

To make the icing, sift together the icing sugar and cinnamon. Beat in enough cider to give a coating consistency. Spread over gingerbread.
Makes 12-16 slices

Flapjacks

4 oz. (½ cup) margarine
4 tablespoons (⅓ cup) golden
  (maple) syrup

1 oz. (3T) soft (light) brown sugar
8 oz. (2¼ cups) rolled oats
pinch of salt

Thoroughly grease an 11 × 7 inch Swiss (jelly) roll tin. Warm the margarine, syrup and sugar in a pan over low heat until the margarine has melted. Stir in the oats and salt.

Press into the prepared tin. Bake above the centre of a moderate oven, 350°F, Gas Mark 4 for 20-25 minutes or until golden brown and firm to the touch. Cut into squares while hot but leave in the tin until cold.
Makes 12-14 squares

Decorated Gingerbread

6 oz. (1½ cups) wholemeal
  (wholewheat) flour
2 teaspoons ground ginger
1 oz. (2T) preserved ginger,
  chopped (optional)
2 oz. (¼ cup) margarine or lard
  (shortening)
2 oz. (⅓ cup) soft (light) brown
  sugar
2 oz. (3T) black treacle (molasses)
2 oz. (3T) golden (maple) syrup

1 teaspoon bicarbonate of soda
  (baking soda)
5 tablespoons (6T) milk, warmed
1 egg, beaten
Icing:
1-2 tablespoons lemon juice
4 oz. (1 cup) icing (confectioners')
  sugar, sifted
1 oz. (2T) preserved ginger,
  chopped (optional)

Line an 11 × 7 inch Swiss (jelly) roll tin with greased greaseproof paper or non-stick parchment. Sift the flour and ground ginger together into a bowl. Add the preserved ginger, if used.

Warm the margarine, sugar, treacle and syrup in a pan over low heat until the margarine has melted. Cool slightly. Dissolve the bicarbonate of soda in the warm milk. Make a well in the centre of the flour and pour in the syrup mixture together with the milk and beaten egg. Beat thoroughly until smooth.

Pour quickly into the prepared tin and bake in the centre of a moderate oven, 350°F, Gas Mark 4 for about 40 minutes or until well-risen and springy to the touch. Leave in the tin for 15 minutes then turn out and cool on a wire rack.

Add enough lemon juice to the icing sugar to give a smooth spreading consistency. Spread over gingerbread and decorate with preserved ginger, if desired. Cut into slices before serving.
Makes about 15 slices

Apricot Upside Down Cake

2 oz. (¼ cup) margarine
4 oz. (⅓ cup) golden (maple)
  syrup
2 oz. (¼ cup) sugar
1 egg, beaten
2 tablespoons (3T) milk
2 oz. (⅔ cup) desiccated
  (shredded) coconut

4 oz. (1 cup) self-raising flour,
  sifted
Topping:
2 oz. (¼ cup) margarine
2 oz. (¼ cup) sugar
8-10 glacé (candied) cherries
14 oz. can apricot halves, drained

Line a 7 or 8 inch round cake tin with greased greaseproof paper or non-stick parchment. Melt the margarine, syrup and sugar in a pan over low heat. Allow to cool, then add the beaten egg and milk. Place the coconut and flour in a mixing bowl and make a well in the centre. Pour in the syrup mixture and beat until smooth.

Cream together the margarine and sugar for the topping. Spread over the base and sides of the prepared tin. Place a cherry in the centre of each apricot half. Arrange apricots, cut side down, in the tin. Top with the cake mixture.

Bake in the centre of a moderate oven, 350°F, Gas Mark 4 for 40-50 minutes or until springy to the touch. Leave in the tin for a few minutes before turning out onto a wire rack to cool.
Makes one 7 or 8 inch round cake

Nutty Bran Cake

4 oz. (1⅔ cups) All-bran
2 oz. (⅓ cup) soft (light) brown
  sugar
6 tablespoons (½ cup) milk
2 oz. (¼ cup) margarine
3 oz. (¼ cup) golden (maple)
  syrup
juice and grated rind of 1 orange

6 oz. (1½ cups) self-raising flour
1 teaspoon ground cinnamon
3 oz. (¾ cup) walnuts, chopped
1 egg, beaten
Topping:
1 tablespoon golden (maple)
  syrup, warmed
1 oz. (¼ cup) walnuts, chopped

Line a 2 lb. loaf tin with greased greaseproof paper or non-stick parchment. Place the All-bran, sugar and milk in a bowl and leave for 30 minutes. Warm the margarine, syrup and orange juice in a pan over low heat.

Sift the flour and cinnamon together into a bowl. Add the walnuts and orange rind. Make a well in the centre of the dry ingredients, add the bran mixture, syrup and egg and beat until smooth.

Turn into the prepared tin and bake in the centre of a moderate oven, 325°F, Gas Mark 3 for 1-1¼ hours or until the cake springs back when pressed gently with the fingers. Turn out and cool on a wire rack. Brush the top with warmed syrup and sprinkle with chopped nuts.
Makes one 2 lb. loaf cake

Mocha Ring

2 oz. (¼ cup) margarine
2 tablespoons (3T) cocoa powder
¼ pint (⅔ cup) milk
2 tablespoons (3T) instant coffee
  powder
4 eggs, separated
6 oz. (¾ cup) castor (superfine)
  sugar
4 oz. (1 cup) self-raising flour,
  sifted
Syrup:
2 oz. (¼ cup) castor (superfine)
  sugar

¼ pint (⅔ cup) water
1 tablespoon instant coffee
  powder
1-2 tablespoons rum or brandy
Icing:
1 tablespoon cocoa powder
2 tablespoons (3T) hot milk
3 oz. (⅓ cup) margarine
6 oz. (1⅓ cups) icing
  (confectioners') sugar, sifted
1 oz. (¼ cup) blanched almonds,
  toasted

Thoroughly grease and flour a 9 inch savarin tin or ring mould. Melt the margarine in a pan over low heat. Blend in the cocoa and milk and bring to the boil, stirring all the time. Stir in the instant coffee. Allow to cool.

Whisk together the egg yolks and sugar until pale and fluffy, then gradually beat in the cooled cocoa mixture. Whisk the egg whites until stiff and quickly but gently fold in, together with the flour.

Turn into the prepared tin and bake in the centre of a moderate oven, 350°F, Gas Mark 4 for 35-45 minutes or until springy to the touch. Leave in the tin for a few minutes before turning out onto a wire rack to cool.

To make the syrup, dissolve the sugar in the water in a pan over low heat. Increase the heat and boil steadily for 3 minutes. Stir in the instant coffee and leave to cool. Add the rum or brandy and carefully spoon the syrup over the cake.

For the icing, blend the cocoa with the milk and leave to cool. Place margarine and sugar in a bowl and add the cocoa mixture. Beat with a wooden spoon until smooth. Spread icing over the cake and mark a pattern with a fork. Decorate with almonds.
Makes one 9 inch ring cake

Walnut and Orange Cake

12 oz. (3 cups) self-raising flour
¼ teaspoon ground cinnamon
3 oz. (½ cup) mixed (candied)
  peel, chopped
3 oz. (¾ cup) walnuts, chopped
3 oz. (½ cup) soft (light) brown
  sugar

3 oz. (⅓ cup) butter
2 tablespoons (3T) golden
  (maple) syrup
2 tablespoons (3T) orange juice
3 eggs, beaten

Line a 2 lb. loaf tin with greased greaseproof paper or non-stick parchment. Sift the flour and cinnamon together into a bowl. Add mixed peel and walnuts.

Warm the sugar, butter and syrup in a pan over low heat until the butter has melted. Stir in the orange juice. Make a well in the centre of the dry ingredients and pour in the syrup. Add the eggs and beat until smooth.

Pour into the prepared tin and bake in the centre of a moderately hot oven, 375°F, Gas Mark 5 for 40-50 minutes or until a skewer, inserted into the centre of the cake, comes out clean. Cool slightly in the tin before turning out onto a wire rack to cool completely.

Makes one 2 lb. loaf cake

Allspice Malt Ring

8 oz. (2 cups) plain (all-purpose)
  flour
1 teaspoon ground allspice
¼ teaspoon bicarbonate of soda
  (baking soda)
2 oz. (½ cup) walnuts, chopped
2 oz. (⅓ cup) dried apricots,
  chopped
2 oz. (3T) golden (maple) syrup
2 tablespoons (3T) malt extract

1 oz. (3T) brown sugar
¼ pint (⅔ cup) milk
Icing and decoration:
4 oz. (1 cup) icing (confectioners')
  sugar, sifted
2 teaspoons hot water
  (approximately)
2 oz. (¼ cup) glacé (candied)
  cherries, quartered

Thoroughly grease and flour an 8 inch ring mould. Sift the flour, allspice and bicarbonate of soda together into a bowl. Stir in the walnuts and apricots.

Warm the syrup, malt and sugar in a pan over low heat. Add the milk. Make a well in the centre of the dry ingredients and pour in the syrup mixture. Beat well to give a smooth, soft dropping consistency.

Pour into the prepared mould and bake in the centre of a moderate oven, 325°F, Gas Mark 3 for 1-1¼ hours or until golden brown and firm. Carefully turn out onto a wire rack to cool.

Combine the icing sugar with enough hot water to give a thick, spreading consistency. Pour over the ring. Decorate with glacé cherries.

Makes one 8 inch ring cake

WHISKED CAKES

Cakes made by the whisking method are very light, due to the large amount of air incorporated into the mixture during whisking. Use an electric hand mixer, rotary or balloon whisk to whisk together the eggs and sugar over a bowl of hot water.

Care must be taken when adding the flour to whisked cake mixtures to ensure there is no loss in volume. Sift the flour at least once and fold in gently but quickly, using a large metal spoon or plastic spatula.

Whisked cakes must be baked as soon as they have been prepared. Fatless sponges will not keep fresh for long and should preferably be eaten on the day of baking.

Fancy Cakes

3 eggs
3 oz. (⅓ cup) castor (superfine)
  sugar
3 oz. (¾ cup) plain (all-purpose)
  flour, sifted
Glacé Icing:
6 oz. (1⅓ cups) icing
  (confectioners') sugar, sifted
1-2 tablespoons hot water
food colouring (optional)

Buttercream:
1½ oz. (3T) butter
3 oz. (⅔ cup) icing (confectioners')
  sugar, sifted
1 teaspoon warm milk
food colouring (optional)
Decoration:
cherries, angelica and nuts

Line an 8 or 9 inch square cake tin with greased greaseproof paper or non-stick parchment.

Whisk eggs and sugar in a warmed bowl over hot water until thick and pale. Remove from heat and continue whisking until cool; the mixture should be very light and thick. Quickly but gently fold in the flour, using a metal spoon.

Turn into prepared tin and bake immediately just above the centre of a moderately hot oven, 375°F, Gas Mark 5 for 20-25 minutes or until the cake springs back when pressed lightly with the fingers. Leave in the tin for 5 minutes before carefully turning out onto a wire rack to cool.

Mix the icing sugar with enough hot water to give a smooth glacé icing, thick enough to coat the back of a spoon. Add colouring, if desired.

To make the buttercream, soften the butter and gradually beat in the icing sugar and milk. The buttercream should be soft enough to pipe. Add colouring, if desired.

Place the cake on a flat surface and cut out shapes of choice. Place on a wire rack with a plate underneath and coat with glacé icing. Decorate with cherries, nuts and angelica. When glacé icing has set, decorate with piped buttercream stars.
Makes 8-10 fancy cakes

Butter Sponge

3 large eggs, separated
3 oz. (⅓ cup) castor (superfine)
  sugar
3 oz. (¾ cup) plain (all-purpose)
  flour, sifted
2 oz. (¼ cup) unsalted (sweet)
  butter, melted
Icing:
2 oz. (2 squares) plain
  (semi-sweet) chocolate

6 tablespoons (½ cup) milk
4 oz. (½ cup) sugar
pinch of salt
1 tablespoon syrup
½ oz. (1T) butter, melted
few drops of vanilla essence
  (extract)
Decoration:
grated chocolate

Line a 7 inch round cake tin with greased greaseproof paper or non-stick parchment. Whisk egg yolks and sugar in a bowl over hot water until pale and fluffy. Fold in half the flour. Whisk egg whites until stiff and fold in gently, using a metal spoon. Pour in the melted butter in a thin stream at the side of the bowl. Fold in the remaining flour. Turn into prepared tin.

Bake in the centre of a moderate oven, 350°F, Gas Mark 4 for 30-35 minutes or until the cake has shrunk slightly from the edge of the tin and springs back when gently pressed with the fingers. Leave in the tin for 5 minutes before turning out onto a wire rack to cool.

Place the chocolate and milk in a pan over a very low heat and stir until the chocolate has dissolved. Add the sugar, salt and syrup and continue stirring over low heat until dissolved. Cook, without stirring, until a sugar thermometer registers 238°F or until a little of the mixture forms a very soft ball when dropped into cold water. Remove from the heat and beat in the butter and vanilla essence. Cool until the icing is thick enough to coat the back of a spoon. Spread over the cake. Sprinkle grated chocolate on top.
Makes one 7 inch round cake

Chocolate and Ginger Swiss Roll

3 large eggs
few drops of vanilla essence
  (extract)
3 oz. (⅓ cup) castor (superfine)
  sugar
3 oz. (¾ cup) plain (all-purpose)
  flour, sifted
2 tablespoons (3T) cocoa powder,
  sifted

1 tablespoon warm water
Filling and decoration:
2 oz. (¼ cup) preserved ginger,
  chopped
¼ pint (⅔ cup) double (heavy)
  cream, whipped
few chocolate buttons

Line a 14 × 10 inch Swiss (jelly) roll tin with greased greaseproof paper or non-stick parchment.

Whisk eggs, vanilla essence and sugar in a bowl over hot water until thick and pale. Remove bowl from heat and continue whisking until the mixture is cold. Gently, but speedily fold in the flour, cocoa and water.

Turn into the prepared tin and bake immediately just above the centre of a moderately hot oven, 400°F, Gas Mark 6 for 10-12 minutes or until the sponge has slightly shrunk from the edges of the tin and springs back when pressed lightly with the fingers.

Turn out onto sugared greaseproof (waxed) paper. Brush lining paper on bottom of sponge with cold water and gently peel off. Trim crispy edges. Make a dent with the back of a knife about ½ inch from the edge on one short side. Beginning on this side, carefully roll up the sponge with the sugared paper inside. Leave to cool, then gently unroll and remove the paper.

Reserve a few pieces of ginger for decoration. Spread the Swiss (jelly) roll with half the whipped cream and the rest of the ginger, then roll up firmly. Place remaining cream in a forcing bag fitted with a star nozzle and decorate Swiss roll with piped cream, ginger and chocolate buttons.
Makes one Swiss (jelly) roll

Lemon Layer Cake

3 eggs
3 oz. (⅓ cup) castor (superfine)
  sugar
3 oz. (¾ cup) plain (all-purpose)
  flour, sifted
finely grated rind of ½ lemon
Filling:
1 oz. (2T) unsalted (sweet) butter
2 oz. (¼ cup) castor (superfine)
  sugar
finely grated rind of ½ lemon

juice of 1 lemon
1 egg, beaten
Glacé icing:
4 oz. (1 cup) icing (confectioners')
  sugar, sifted
juice of ½ lemon
few drops of yellow food
  colouring, (optional)
Decoration:
thinly pared rind of 1 lemon,
  boiled and shredded

Line a 7 inch round cake tin with greased greaseproof paper or non-stick parchment. Whisk eggs and sugar in a warmed bowl over hot water until pale and thick. Remove bowl from hot water. Continue whisking until cool. Quickly and lightly fold in the flour and lemon rind, using a metal spoon. Turn into prepared tin and smooth the top.

Bake just above the centre of a moderate oven, 350°F, Gas Mark 4 for 25-30 minutes until golden brown and springy to the touch. Allow to cool slightly in the tin before turning out onto a wire rack to cool.

To make the filling, melt the butter in a basin over hot water. Add the sugar, lemon rind and juice. Strain in the beaten egg. Stir over hot water until the mixture thickens enough to coat the back of a spoon. Remove basin from hot water and allow to cool.

To make the glacé icing, beat the icing sugar with enough lemon juice to give a smooth icing, thick enough to coat the back of a spoon. Add a few drops of colouring, if liked.

Slice the cake into 3 layers. Sandwich together with lemon filling. Spread glacé icing over the top and sprinkle with shredded lemon rind.
Makes one 7 inch round cake

Intriguing Chocolate Cake

5 large eggs
few drops of vanilla essence
  (extract)
5 oz. (⅔ cup) castor (superfine)
  sugar
5 oz. (1¼ cups) plain (all-purpose)
  flour, sifted
1 teaspoon baking powder
1 tablespoon cocoa powder, sifted

Icing and decoration:
5 oz. (⅔ cup) margarine, softened
9 oz. (2 cups) icing (confectioners')
  sugar, sifted
4 tablespoons (⅓ cup) cocoa
  powder, sifted
1 tablespoon hot water
1-2 oz. (1-2 squares) plain
  (semi-sweet) chocolate, grated

Line a 14 × 10 inch Swiss (jelly) roll tin and an 8 inch round cake tin with greased greaseproof paper or non-stick parchment.

Whisk eggs, vanilla essence and sugar together in a bowl over hot water until thick and pale. Remove bowl from hot water and whisk until cool. Sift the flour and baking powder together. Fold into the whisked mixture, using a metal tablespoon.

Place half the mixture in the prepared Swiss roll tin. Quickly fold the cocoa powder into the remaining mixture. Place in the prepared cake tin. Bake cakes just above the centre of a moderately hot oven, 400°F, Gas Mark 6 for 10-15 minutes or until the sponges feel springy to the touch. Turn out onto a wire rack to cool.

To make the icing, cream the margarine and icing sugar together until light and fluffy. Set aside 2 tablespoons (3T) of the icing. Blend the cocoa with the hot water and beat into the rest of the icing.

Cut the Swiss (jelly) roll into 5 lengthwise strips. Split the chocolate cake in half and spread one cut surface with chocolate icing. Spread each of the 5 strips of sponge with chocolate icing.

Roll the strips round each other on the iced cake layer to resemble the end of a large Swiss roll. Place the other chocolate cake layer on top. Cover sides with chocolate icing and roll in grated chocolate.

Cover the top with chocolate icing. Soften the reserved plain icing with a little hot water and pipe straight lines about 1 inch apart on top of the cake. Make a feather pattern by drawing a skewer in alternate directions across the lines. Pipe remaining chocolate icing around the edge of the cake.

Makes one 8 inch round cake

Black Forest Gâteau

3 oz. (¾ cup) self-raising flour
1 oz. (¼ cup) cocoa powder
4 eggs
4 oz. (½ cup) castor (superfine)
 sugar
1 tablespoon warm water
Filling and decoration:
15 oz. can stoned (pitted) black
 (bing) cherries

2 teaspoons cornflour (cornstarch)
4 tablespoons (⅓ cup) Kirsch
½ pint (1¼ cups) whipping cream,
 whipped or 2 packets Dream
 Topping made up with ½ pint
 (1¼ cups) milk, as directed
3 oz. (3 squares) plain
 (semi-sweet) chocolate
chocolate curls (optional)

Line two 9 inch sandwich tins (cake layer pans) with greased greaseproof paper or non-stick parchment. Sift the flour and cocoa together. Whisk eggs and sugar in a warmed bowl over hot water until the mixture is pale and fluffy. Remove from heat and continue whisking until the mixture is cold. Gently, but quickly, fold in the flour, cocoa and water, using a large metal spoon.

Divide the mixture between the prepared tins and bake just above the centre of a moderate oven, 350°F, Gas Mark 4 for 25-35 minutes or until the cakes spring back when lightly pressed with the fingers. Turn out and cool on a wire rack.

Drain the juice from the cherries and make up to ¼ pint (⅔ cup) with water. Blend a little of this liquid with the cornflour, then stir in the remainder. Bring to the boil, stirring all the time. Add the cherries and allow to cool.

Place one sponge layer on a serving plate and sprinkle with 2 tablespoons (3T) of the Kirsch. Cover with a layer of whipped cream or Dream Topping and most of the cherries. Place the other sponge layer on top.

Melt the plain chocolate in a basin over hot water. Spread the melted chocolate thinly on a sheet of greaseproof (waxed) paper and leave until set. Using a sharp knife, cut the chocolate into triangles.

Cover the top of the sponge with a layer of whipped cream or Dream Topping and decorate the edge with piped swirls of cream or Topping and the chocolate triangles. Pile the remaining cherries into the centre and sprinkle the chocolate curls, if used, over the gâteau.
Makes one 9 inch round gâteau

Note: To make chocolate curls, shave off pieces of chocolate using a potato peeler.

BLACK FOREST GÂTEAU *(Photograph: Bird's Dessert Bureau)*

Walnut Cake

4 eggs, separated
3 oz. (⅓ cup) castor (superfine)
  sugar
2 oz. (1 cup) fresh breadcrumbs
2 oz. (½ cup) walnuts, finely
  grated
Filling:
2 tablespoons (3T) milk

2 oz. (½ cup) walnuts, finely
  grated
2 oz. (¼ cup) butter
4 oz. (1 cup) icing (confectioners')
  sugar, sifted
1 tablespoon rum
castor (superfine) sugar for dusting

Line an 8 inch round cake tin with greased greaseproof paper or non-stick parchment. Whisk egg yolks and sugar until pale and fluffy. Blend in the breadcrumbs and walnuts. Beat the egg whites until stiff and gently fold into the mixture, using a metal spoon.

Turn into the prepared tin and bake in the centre of a moderate oven, 325°F, Gas Mark 3 for 25-35 minutes or until the cake springs back when pressed lightly with the fingers. Turn out onto a wire rack to cool.

To make the filling, warm the milk with the walnuts in a pan over low heat. Cool. Cream butter and icing sugar together until pale and fluffy. Beat in the walnut mixture and rum.

Cut the cake into 2 layers and sandwich together with walnut cream. Sprinkle castor sugar on top.
Makes one 8 inch round cake

Swiss Roll

3 large eggs
3 oz. (⅓ cup) castor (superfine)
  sugar
3 oz. (¾ cup) plain (all-purpose)
  flour

1 tablespoon warm water
jam for filling
sugar for dusting

Line a 12 × 8 inch Swiss (jelly) roll tin with greased greaseproof paper or non-stick parchment. Whisk the eggs and sugar in a bowl over hot water until the mixture is pale and thick enough to leave a trail.

Remove the bowl from heat and continue whisking until cold. Gently fold in half of the flour, using a metal tablespoon. Carefully fold in the remaining flour and water. Turn the mixture quickly into the prepared tin.

Bake immediately just above the centre of a hot oven, 425°F, Gas Mark 7 for 8-10 minutes or until golden brown and springy to the touch.

Have ready a sheet of sugared greaseproof paper or non-stick parchment. Turn the sponge out onto the sugared paper and carefully peel off the lining paper. Trim away the crisp edges. Spread with jam to within ½ inch of the edges. Roll up firmly. Cool on a wire rack. Before serving, sprinkle with sugar.
Makes one Swiss (jelly) roll

Easter Cake

3 eggs
3 oz. (⅓ cup) castor (superfine)
  sugar
3 oz. (¾ cup) self-raising flour,
  sifted
1½ oz. (3T) butter, melted and
  cooled

Icing:
3 oz. (3 squares) cooking
  chocolate
4 oz. (½ cup) castor (superfine)
  sugar

4 tablespoons (⅓ cup) water
2 egg yolks, beaten
4 oz. (½ cup) butter, softened
1 teaspoon coffee essence (strong
  black coffee)

Praline:
1 oz. (2T) sugar
1 oz. (¼ cup) blanched almonds,
  coarsely chopped

Line an 8 inch round cake tin with greased greaseproof paper or non-stick parchment. Whisk the eggs and sugar together in a bowl over hot water until thick and pale. Remove from the heat and continue whisking until cool. Gently, but quickly fold in half the flour. Pour in the melted butter in a steady stream at the side of the bowl. Fold in the remaining flour.

Turn into the prepared tin and bake just above the centre of a moderate oven, 350°F, Gas Mark 4 for 30-35 minutes or until the cake springs back when pressed lightly with the fingers. Turn out and cool on a wire rack.

Melt the chocolate for the icing in a bowl over hot water. Dissolve the sugar in the water in a pan over low heat. Increase the heat and boil until a temperature of 230°F is reached or until a little of the cooled mixture will form a thread when drawn between the thumb and forefinger. Gradually pour onto the egg yolks, whisking constantly. Beat in the softened butter, melted chocolate and coffee essence.

To make the praline, place the sugar and almonds in a pan over low heat and stir until the sugar melts. Continue cooking, stirring constantly until the mixture is golden brown. Turn onto greased greaseproof (waxed) paper and leave to harden. Crush the praline with a rolling pin.

Slice the cake into 2 layers and sandwich together with some of the icing. Coat the top and sides with icing. Press the coarsely crushed praline round the sides. Decorate the top with piped stars of chocolate icing.

Makes one 8 inch round cake

Mandarin Gâteau

3 eggs

3 oz. (⅓ cup) castor (superfine) sugar

3 oz. (¾ cup) plain (all-purpose) flour, sifted

Filling and decoration:

3 tablespoons (¼ cup) apricot jam

½ pint (1 ¼ cups) double (heavy) cream, whipped or 2 packets Dream Topping made up with ½ pint (1 ¼ cups) milk, as directed

3-4 oz. (¾-1 cup) walnuts, chopped

11oz. can mandarin oranges

Line two 7 inch sandwich tins (cake layer pans) with greased greaseproof paper or non-stick parchment.

Whisk eggs and sugar in a bowl over hot water until pale and fluffy. Remove from heat and continue whisking until the mixture is cool. Gently fold in the flour, using a large metal spoon.

Divide mixture evenly between the prepared tins and bake just above the centre of a moderately hot oven, 375°F, Gas Mark 5 for 20-25 minutes or until the cakes spring back when pressed lightly with the fingers. Allow to cool slightly in the tins before turning out onto a wire rack to cool completely.

Sandwich cake layers together with 2 tablespoons (3T) jam and a layer of whipped cream or Dream Topping. Spread the sides of the cake with whipped cream or Dream Topping and roll in the chopped nuts.

Drain the mandarins, reserving 3 tablespoons (¼ cup) mandarin juice. Sprinkle over the cake. Spread a layer of Dream Topping over the top of the cake. Arrange mandarins on top. Heat remaining 1 tablespoon jam with a little water. Sieve and brush over the mandarins. Decorate with remaining cream or Dream Topping.

Makes one 7 inch round gâteau

RUBBED-IN CAKES

Cakes made by the rubbing-in method require firm margarine or butter. It is preferable to use the fat straight from the refrigerator. For ease of preparation, coarsely grate the fat or cut it into small pieces then rub this into the flour using the fingertips. The mixture should resemble fine breadcrumbs before other ingredients are added.

Ginger Cake

8 oz. (2 cups) self-raising flour
4 oz. (½ cup) butter
4 oz. (½ cup) castor (superfine) sugar

3 oz. (⅓ cup) preserved ginger, chopped
1 egg
5 tablespoons (6T) milk

Line a 7 inch round cake tin with greased greaseproof paper or non-stick parchment. Sift the flour into a bowl. Cut up the butter and rub into the flour, using the fingertips. Stir in the sugar. Add the chopped ginger. Beat the egg with the milk and stir into the mixture.

Turn into the prepared tin. Bake in the centre of a moderate oven, 350°F, Gas Mark 4 for about 50 minutes or until a skewer, inserted into the centre of the cake, comes out clean.

Leave in the tin for about 15 minutes before turning out onto a wire rack to cool.

Makes one 7 inch round cake

Banana Slices

8 oz. (2¼ cups) rolled oats
8 oz. (2 cups) self-raising flour
4 oz. (½ cup) margarine
8 oz. (1⅓ cups) soft (light) brown sugar

2 eggs, beaten
4 bananas, sliced

Thoroughly grease an 8 inch square loose-bottomed cake tin. Place the oats and flour in a bowl. Cut up the margarine and rub into the dry ingredients, using the fingertips. Stir in the sugar then add the beaten eggs. Mix thoroughly.

Press one half of the mixture into the prepared tin. Arrange the bananas over the mixture. Spread the remaining mixture on top.

Bake above the centre of a moderate oven, 350°F, Gas Mark 4 for 25-30 minutes until golden brown. Cut into squares while still warm but leave in the tin until cold.

Makes 10-12 slices

Crunchy Apple Cake

4 oz. (1 cup) self-raising flour
2 oz. (½ cup) ground almonds
3 oz. (⅓ cup) butter
2 oz. (⅓ cup) soft (light) brown
  sugar
1 teaspoon lemon juice
1 small egg (approximately),
  beaten
Filling:
1 lb. (4 cups) cooking apples,
  peeled and diced

3 oz. (½ cup) soft (light) brown
  sugar
1 teaspoon lemon juice
Topping:
3 oz. (¾ cup) self-raising flour
1 teaspoon ground cinnamon
2 oz. (¼ cup) butter
2 oz. (⅓ cup) soft (light) brown
  sugar

Grease an 8 inch round loose-bottomed cake tin. Sift together the flour and 1 oz (¼ cup) ground almonds. Cut up the butter and rub into the dry ingredients, using the fingertips. Stir in the sugar. Mix in the lemon juice and enough beaten egg to give a stiff dough.

Press the mixture into the prepared tin. Sprinkle with the remaining ground almonds and chill. Combine the apples, sugar and lemon juice for the filling. Arrange over the cake base.

To make the topping, sift the flour and cinnamon together into a bowl. Cut up the butter and rub into the dry ingredients, using the fingertips. Stir in the sugar. Sprinkle the topping over the cake. Bake in the centre of a moderate oven, 350°F, Gas Mark 4 for 1-1¼ hours until the topping is golden brown. Leave in the tin for 10 minutes before turning out onto a wire rack to cool.
Makes one 8 inch round cake

Date Slices

4 oz. (1 cup) wholemeal
  (wholewheat) flour
4 oz. (1 cup) rolled oats
4 oz. (½ cup) margarine
2 oz. (⅓ cup) soft (light) brown
  sugar

Filling:
8 oz. (1¼ cups) stoned (pitted)
  dates, chopped
juice and grated rind of 1 lemon

Grease a shallow 11 × 7 inch baking tin. Place the flour and oats in a bowl. Coarsely grate the margarine and rub into the dry ingredients, using the fingertips. Stir in the sugar. Press half the mixture into the prepared tin.

Place the chopped dates, lemon rind and juice in a small pan with a little water. Simmer until the dates are soft. Drain thoroughly. Spread over the mixture in the tin. Spoon the remaining mixture over the dates. Bake above the centre of a moderate oven, 350°F, Gas Mark 4 for 25-35 minutes until lightly browned.

Cut into 12-14 slices while still warm but leave to cool in the tin.
Makes 12-14 slices

Iced Fruit Cake

8 oz. (2 cups) self-raising flour
4 oz. (½ cup) butter
4 oz. (⅔ cup) soft (light) brown
  sugar
6 oz. (1 cup) mixed dried fruit
2 oz. (¼ cup) glacé (candied)
  cherries, chopped
2 eggs
4 tablespoons (⅓ cup) milk
3 tablespoons (¼ cup) apricot
  jam, warmed and sieved
1 lb. almond paste, see page 43

Icing:
1 oz. (2T) margarine
1 tablespoon lemon juice
12 oz. (2⅔ cups) icing
  (confectioners') sugar
  (approximately), sifted
few drops of yellow food colouring
Decoration:
1 egg white
1 teaspoon cold water
15-20 primroses, stalks removed
castor sugar for dusting

Line a 7 inch round cake tin with greased greaseproof paper or non-stick parchment. Sift the flour into a bowl and rub in the butter, using the fingertips. Stir in the sugar then add the dried fruit and cherries. Beat eggs with milk and stir into the mixture.

Turn into the prepared tin and bake in the centre of a moderate oven, 350°F, Gas Mark 4 for 50-55 minutes or until a skewer, inserted into the centre of the cake, comes out clean. Leave in the tin for 5 minutes before turning out onto a wire rack to cool.

To make the icing, place the margarine and lemon juice in a saucepan and heat gently until the margarine has melted. Add 4 oz. (1 cup) icing sugar and cook, stirring, over low heat for 2 minutes.

Remove from the heat and add another 4 oz. (1 cup) icing sugar and the yellow colouring. Beat thoroughly with a wooden spoon. Continue adding icing sugar, beating constantly, until the icing is the consistency of a soft dough. Turn onto a board, dusted with icing sugar, and knead until smooth. Roll out the icing to a circle, large enough to cover the cake. Mould the icing over the cake, smoothing the sides.

To make the decoration, beat the egg white with water. Dip the primroses carefully into the egg white then into castor sugar. Leave to dry on kitchen paper. Decorate the cake with the frosted primroses.
Makes one 7 inch round cake

ICED FRUIT CAKE, FANCY CAKES *(page 74)*
(Photograph: British Sugar Bureau)

Chocolate Cake

7 oz. (1¾ cups) self-raising flour
pinch of salt
1 oz. (¼ cup) cocoa powder
4 oz. (½ cup) margarine
8 oz. (1 cup) castor (superfine)
  sugar
2 eggs
5 tablespoons (6T) evaporated
  milk
5 tablespoons (6T) water

Icing:
2½ oz. (¼ cup + 1T) margarine
4 tablespoons (⅓ cup) cocoa
  powder
8 oz. (1¾ cups) icing
  (confectioners') sugar, sifted
3 tablespoons (¼ cup) hot milk
1 teaspoon vanilla essence
  (extract)

Grease and flour two 8 inch sandwich tins (cake layer pans). Sift together the flour, salt and cocoa. Cut up the margarine and rub into mixture, using the fingertips. Stir in the sugar. Beat the eggs with the evaporated milk and water and add to the dry ingredients. Beat with a wooden spoon until the mixture is smooth. Pour into the prepared tins.

Bake above the centre of a moderate oven, 350°F, Gas Mark 4 for about 35 minutes or until the cake springs back when pressed lightly with the fingers. Turn out onto a wire rack to cool.

Melt the margarine for the icing. Blend in the cocoa and gradually stir in the icing sugar, milk and vanilla essence. Beat until smooth and thick. Sandwich the cakes together with icing. Cover the top of the cake with the remaining icing.

Makes one 8 inch round cake

INDEX

INDEX